Knowing your own darkness is the best method for dealing with the darknesses of other people.

— C. G. Jung

So many unanswered questions live within me [that I am] afraid to uncover them—because of the blasphemy—If there be God—please forgive me—When I try to raise my thoughts to Heaven—there is such convicting emptiness that those very thoughts return like sharp knives and hurt my very soul.—I am told God loves me—and yet the reality of darkness and coldness and emptiness is so great that nothing touches my soul.

— Mother Teresa of Calcutta

Knowing Darkness

On Skepticism, Melancholy,
Friendship, and God

ADDISON HODGES HART

Ben & Selwyn:
When you're down
and blue, & it seems like everything
is bleak & hellish, this little book
is sure to put a smile back on
your faces and a warm,
"Thomas Kincaid" feeling in
your hearts —
Addison

William B. Eerdmans Publishing Company
Grand Rapids, Michigan / Cambridge, U.K.

Published 2009 by

Wm. B. Eerdmans Publishing Co.

2140 Oak Industrial Drive N.E., Grand Rapids, Michigan 49505 /

P.O. Box 163, Cambridge CB3 9PU U.K.

www.eerdmans.com

Printed in the United States of America

14 13 12 11 10 09   7 6 5 4 3 2 1

ISBN 978-0-8028-6344-7

Unless otherwise noted, the Scripture quotations in this publication are from the Revised Standard Version of the Bible.

The author and publisher acknowledge permission to reprint copyrighted materials granted by the publishers listed on page 136.

Dedicated to the memory of

JOHN MICHAEL MARCIN

1954-2001

Contents

Chapter One

INTRODUCTION
Walking by Faith, Not by Sight: The Darkness of Mother Teresa

A S HER private journals and letters reveal, Blessed Teresa of Calcutta suffered terribly for decades. It was an interior suffering, one which the world could not see or, if it could, would not have understood. "In my soul I feel just that terrible pain of loss, of God not wanting me — of God not being God — of God not existing."[1] She wrote these disturbing words in 1959, and the appalling fact of the matter is that she remained in this state of mind until the end of her life in 1997. "If I ever become a saint," she lamented, "I will surely be one of 'darkness.'"[2]

There is no need to acquaint ourselves with the life story of Mother Teresa. It is well documented, and she

---

1. Mother Teresa, quoted in *The New York Times*, 23 Aug. 2007.
2. Mother Teresa, quoted in *The New York Times*, 5 Sept. 2007.

was virtually regarded as a canonized saint during her lifetime. No one doubted her faith, and it was visible to all as she and her Missionaries of Charity served "the poorest of the poor" and "Christ in his distressing disguise," first in Calcutta and then all over the world, wherever extreme poverty and disease held sway. She was almost an object of adoration.

And yet, she did what she did while enduring deep darkness of mind. She even doubted at times the existence of God.

As one might expect, there followed upon the public announcement in 2007 of the contents and publication of her private papers (the nature of which had been known since 2002) some crowing in *Newsweek* from her bibulous erstwhile detractor, Christopher Hitchens, whose excoriating book about her was entitled, with the vulgarest vitriol, *The Missionary Position,* and whose later bizarre performance during the ABC coverage of her funeral said far more about him than about her. As an advocate of Enlightenment atheism, one can recognize his pleasure at finding that Mother Teresa was a closet atheist all along — a woman who was maneuvered by an unscrupulous church to use her lost, phony "faith" to advance an agenda and to save face. Sam Harris, another champion of atheism, chimed in for an Internet column for *Newsweek* and *The Washington Post,* saying that she suffered from "run-of-the-mill depression" and noting that she accused herself of "hypocrisy" (a self-judgment with which he's happy to concur).[3] (What, by the way, is "run-of-the-mill depression"? And who — church official or not — would bother to deny that Mother Teresa suffered from "depression" anyway? Is there some stigma about depression itself, and has it no place in the context of faith? How on earth would Sam Harris know? And who is Sam Harris to deem anyone's depression as "run-of-the-mill"? Just what abundance of ignorance and hubris can be packed into a simple phrase is surely illustrated by his magnificently stupid remark.) Anyway, as in just about everything else they write about religion, Hitchens and Harris don't know what they're talking about — literally.

"Darkness" of an interior kind, and even a sort of "atheism," are not inimical to faith, and certainly not to Christianity or Judaism. "The dark night of the soul" and "the dark night of the spirit," time-honored phrases that come from the writings of the sixteenth-century Spanish Carmelite mystic St. John of the Cross, remind us that the way of Christian faith is not one of light only, but also of obscurity. St. John describes the "dark nights" as mystical

3. Sam Harris, Internet column: http://newsweek.washington post.com.

states through which the proficient must pass in order to know God as he truly is. To do this, we must challenge even what we think is "God," maybe even annihilate it — a smashing of idols fashioned in our own likenesses. *Whatever* God is (St. Thomas Aquinas, one recalls, began his *Summa* famously with the question *What* is God?, not *Who* is God?), the answer must be approached in darkness, a form of "a-theism," a series of *nada, nada, nada.* This aspect of Christian "revelation" is much older than St. John of the Cross, of course. In fact, it's older than Christianity.

But, to return to Mother Teresa of Calcutta: in her "confessions" we discover that, for her, "darkness" profoundly involved two things that often Christians are shallowly warned against: melancholy and skepticism. To *feel* a "terrible pain of loss, of God not wanting me" is a depressive feeling indeed. It is the pain of *melancholy,* a state of mind verging on despair. To *think* "of God not being God — of God not existing" is to experience the challenge to the intellect — a necessary one? — of *skepticism.* And, recall, this was Blessed Teresa of Calcutta who said this, not someone typically associated in people's minds with *doubt.* But, undeniably, she wrote, "I find no words to express the depths of the darkness."[4]

---

4. Mother Teresa, quoted by James Martin in *The New York Times,* 29 Aug. 2007.

Walking by Faith, Not by Sight

AMONG THE many things we can learn (or, better, re-learn) from the life of Mother Teresa, then, one surprising discovery is this: There is room for both skepticism and deep melancholy, for "darkness," in the life of faith. Christians who find these perplexing and troublesome things occupying a place in their minds should not be ashamed of them.

What follows in this book are interlaced reflections on both melancholy and skepticism, and finally reflections on the need, with respect to these, for genuine human friendship in the life of faith. Among Christians, as I suggested above, melancholy and skepticism are frequently derided and discouraged as attitudinal flaws. However, given the idea that there is value in the "darkness" of the "dark nights," isn't it just possible that both melancholy and skepticism are better understood as components of authentic faith, at least for some? A case may certainly be made that they serve as sharpeners of the intellect in the lives of many believers, and are not necessarily the faith-threatening defects they so often are caricatured as being.

I admit right up front that the words *melancholy* and *skepticism* are archaic. I like archaic words. Apart from that, though, I find that in some cases archaic terms are useful precisely because they don't carry along with them the baggage of modern tastes and prejudices found in contemporary terminology and neologisms.

Instead of the much more interesting word *melancholy,* we use the literally flattening word *depression* nowadays. *Depression* suggests to us something to be treated in a clinic, hateful to that supposedly "normal" sense of "happiness" which — as some of our popular media sages tell us — we ought to possess in abundance and promote and (no matter how impracticable it really is for us) practice. This is implicitly to reduce *feeling* (not simply to be confused with "emotions") to the hygienic realm, the quantifiable, measurable, adjustable, and treatable. But "depression" may in many circumstances really be far more than this, even when it justifiably does require medical intervention.

To be sure, *melancholy* has from ancient times been considered a "disease" of the emotions; but mainly in the pristine sense that it is a *dis-ease,* something that leaves us feeling low and comfortless. It should never be too easily dismissed as utterly invaluable to us, something only to be escaped. It may "hurt," but it also may in fact teach us wisdom, and its causes may be real, objective, and impossible to write off. To say it bluntly, there may be real reason why we sometimes feel like hell and want our life to end. There may be real reason why such an emotional condition may linger and flatten us to the ground or make us want to scream internally like Munch's man on the bridge (a great painting sadly now almost relegated to a visual cliché, which it most definitely is not).

Such unsparing notions aside, the definition of *melancholy* which I assume throughout this book is "a feeling of thoughtful sadness." More on that will appear subsequently in the chapter on the book of Ecclesiastes. I want only to say here that to be completely devoid of melancholy in today's world — a world rife with terrorism, war, a multitude of addictions, lack of moral direction, starvation, exploitation, poverty, pornography, abortion, senseless violence (think of Columbine, think of Virginia Tech), vandalism, etcetera, etcetera — is to be lacking something vital to common humanity, whether one is overtly religious or not. It is to lack *feeling* in the most basic sense. If one understands that Mother Teresa's own "darkness" was directly related to these somber facts of human life, conditions she faced daily and unblinkingly, one can also begin to understand, or at least intuit, how this was inevitably related to her faith.

Anything calling itself "faith" that sets itself against the essential human feeling that engenders melancholy is in fact a fraud. Even when melancholy becomes a malady, there are few things more intolerable, tyrannical, and oppressive than the inane injunction that "Thou shalt smile." When this absurd dictum goes on to get mixed up with mass-market religious drivel, such cheerfulness and baffling optimism are enough to drive a thoughtful believer to the brink of disbelief or even despair.

Thank the Good Lord, then, for the safer alternative of "faithful skepticism" — and that is no oxymoron.

Skepticism, of course, is likewise a misunderstood word, usually looked upon in religious circles with disfavor. It conjures up images of squint-eyed old bastards, disillusioned, derisive of religion, not given to suffering fools or anybody else either gladly or reluctantly. Perhaps it conjures up images of Christopher Hitchens bloviating about Mother Teresa's record during her funeral cortège or debating with the Reverend Al Sharpton (the last a wondrous mismatch to behold).

But, be that as it may, skepticism is wrongly considered to be synonymous with "doubt," akin to blasphemy, and a singularly unhealthy frame of mind to bring along with one to church. Some might very well think it best to leave skepticism outside the door and proceed docilely and brainlessly to one's pew, but in fact skepticism has every good reason to be in church. Neither is skepticism grumpiness or cynicism.

It possesses a place of distinction as a laudable quality which keeps religion honest, obliging us to have our eyes open and our brains functioning, making sure that good sense isn't stifled by claptrap, status, fakery, and mummery.

Again, skepticism is precisely the frame of mind we

should adopt toward a great deal of what we see and hear around us in the religious context, just as in the political, social, and economic spheres. Bombarded as we are by tripe, idiocy, propaganda, lying, "humor," and hubris — in other words, "sound bites" — we are fools if we aren't skeptics at some level. The true skeptic is someone with faith at his core, or perhaps the person with authentic faith is a skeptic at his core; because otherwise he will be a stooge, a patsy, a "good soldier," or else a nihilist and a mental black hole. Those who have the name of "skeptic" today are frequently those who, over against religion, want us to buy the same old repeatedly disproved poppycock offered since the "Enlightenment" — some sort of unquestioning blind faith in rationalism, "progress," and this or that economic or political theory. They aren't skeptics, though, but just the latest batch of ideologues, just as potentially totalitarian and fundamentalist as any of the religious fanatics they deplore.

Skepticism is the intellectual correlate of melancholy: a direct consequence of distress or dissatisfaction. It is the form intelligence takes when it has been egged on to scrutinize things more sharply and critically. In the Christian context, this has usually meant an increasing avoidance of accepting the neat packages provided by unthinking biblicism, dogmatism, traditionalism (not to be confused with *tradition* — a point made by the late historian of theology Jaroslav Pelikan when he defined *tradition* as "the living faith of the dead," and *traditionalism* as "the dead faith of the living"), moralism (not to be confused with *morality*), or so-called liberalism.

Like a skilled butcher, skepticism trims away the unnecessary and unwholesome fat that lards and cakes faith and consequently clogs our spiritual arteries. Faith isn't fantasy or superstition or gullibility; it isn't meant to be soft and sweet, nor is it meant to degenerate into devotional and liturgical escapism. Again, faith should not be supplanted by scholastic theological nit-picking or some vast and heavy octopus-pulp of canonical legalism and moralism. Faith is primarily relational, sometimes gritty, and meant to be engaged with the world as Jesus was. There's a genuine place in the household of faith for the work of skepticism. It eliminates, or at least reduces, the excesses and potential nonsense of religion.

TURNING TO the Christian Bible, are melancholy and skepticism perhaps regarded there as arrantly "sinful" attitudes? How, if at all, are these things dealt with in these seminal texts of Christian faith? Would Mother Teresa, for instance, have found herself encouraged or chastised by the words of sacred Scripture in the matter of her darkness and doubts?

To give a very brief answer here, the Scriptures in

their various ancient, "pre-modern" ways depict neither melancholy nor skepticism as good or bad in themselves; rather, they are to be morally judged in relationship to their circumstances and uses. Alongside the biblical injunctions to adhere, as the normative standard of faith, to what I will call in these pages "conventional piety," the Scriptures also present a much more complex and variegated interaction with God. On the level of adult faith, nothing is monochromic or monolithic when the canon is taken as a whole. The approach to God includes uncertainties of doubt and darkness, and melancholy and skepticism are unapologetically present in these holiest books of Christianity and Judaism.

So, in later chapters, I will look at some of the biblical texts where this can more easily be seen.

I intend to do this especially with the help of two rather tough and freethinking biblical figures: the strange and shadowy sage known only as "the Preacher" — Qoheleth, or "Ecclesiastes" — and the long-suffering Job. I will turn, in other words, to two Old Testament books, significant for their shock value (assuming the reader pays attention to them sufficiently to be shocked), to illuminate the positive qualities of both melancholy and skepticism. There will be no attempt on my part to provide extensive commentary on either book. I will only glance cursorily at each of them for the light they shed on the subjects at hand.

Not only will the place of skepticism and melancholy in faith be considered below, but also the need for genuine human friendship among Christians. I say *genuine* human friendship because not all acquaintances — no matter how "friendly" or spiritual or Christian — qualify as *friendship* in the most critical sense.

At first I had no intention of addressing this topic, but as I read through both Ecclesiastes and Job, I perceived in these books the hints of longing for genuine human friendship, and the impact the lack of it had on the characters of Qoheleth and Job. Each of these books has something to say about friendship. Qoheleth may have suffered from its absence in his life, and he also appears possibly to have suffered from a failure in "romantic" love (or so some have speculated, I believe with good reason). Job has "friends," and also a wife, who prove utterly insensitive to his agonies. It should be obvious to anyone that within the context of great suffering — external or internal — there is real need for the supportive love of true friends. It is, I stress, a *need*. When it is lacking, melancholy becomes either just scantly bearable or else completely unbearable, and any consequent skepticism soon degenerates into bitterness. The books of Ecclesiastes and Job implicitly beg the question of this need.

Jesus had some things to say on the matter of friendship, particularly in the fourth Gospel. For him, self-sacrificing friendship was "the greatest love" (John 15:13). Certainly sorrow is linked to the subject of friendship in the Gospels at the tomb of Lazarus, in Gethsemane, on the shore of Tiberias, and elsewhere. Skepticism, as described in these pages, is also connected to the sort of friendship Jesus desires, particularly if one takes into account those sharp-edged dominical teachings that never allow his disciples — his friends — to become complacent or to fall back on conventionalities. Jesus is quite tough on them, pushing them to "see," "hear," and think hard about what he's doing and saying. But all of this is so they may become his *friends,* those to whom he reveals everything. They are no longer to remain just "servants," those who know nothing of any real depth about him or what he does (John 15:14-15).

Faith is maintained in relationship to those we have grown to love and trust, whose support upholds us. Genuine friendship is like "iron sharpening iron" (Prov. 27:17). But, again, it should be *genuine* friendship, something tested and sure. Not every passing acquaintance is friendship; nor is friendship mere socializing. It certainly isn't a euphemism for a sexual relationship. As the twelfth-century Cistercian abbot St. Aelred of Rievaulx pointed out in his work of the same name, true friendship is "*spiritual* friendship." In other words, it is a uniting of minds and hearts at a deep level, not a superficial one;

and the deepest level is the place where the soul is intimately related to God. If friends are united at that most unspoiled point, there and there only do we find something of permanent value, and there we have a relationship worthy of the name of "friendship."

It seemed natural to me, therefore, that an extended reflection on melancholy and skepticism should finally touch on the subject of friendship in Christ as well. All three are rudimentary and integral to human life, immediately interrelated, and therefore part of faith.

So, THIS BOOK is about darkness and "dark nights." It takes seriously the sort of struggle within faith that includes, in Mother Teresa's words, that "terrible pain of loss," in which a person "walks by faith, not by sight" (2 Cor. 5:7) — but does so, paradoxically, because the very light of faith itself seems to have been extinguished. In this darkness the presence of one's true friends becomes all the more precious and vital.

What follows, then, is an interwoven succession of meditations, not a systematic treatment of anything (for which I have something of an aversion temperamentally). The next two chapters will discuss in turn more fully the subjects of skepticism and melancholy. The two chapters after that will look into the books of Ecclesiastes and Job for insights into these. Then there will be a dialogue in the old-fashioned Socratic sense (with a nod to St. Aelred of Rievaulx) on the subject of "spiritual friendship." Lastly, there will be a "Concluding Unscientific Postscript."

Chapter Two

Faith and Skepticism

No ADULT's faith can possibly do without a dash or more of skepticism in it. Not doubt, not cynicism, but skepticism. We are not called to be gullible, witless, and dull as cattle. Being a "sheep" of the Good Shepherd was never intended to suggest the expected level of a Christian's intelligence. The Eastern Church's liturgies have wisely tended to refer to Christians as "rational sheep," and one assumes this is so for this very reason. Stupidity — which has nothing to do with one's I.Q. or the amount of information (or *dis*information) one has imbibed — is not esteemed highly by Christ, even if "childlikeness" is (and "childlikeness" means that one is *teachable* — that is to say, possesses basic intelligence and has a will to learn): "And when Jesus saw that [the scribe] answered wisely [or, intelligently], he said to him,

'You are not far from the kingdom of God'" (Mark 12:34).
St. Paul exhorts his readers to present to God "reasonable
[*logiken*] worship" and to have their "mind [*noos*]" renewed (Rom. 12:1-2). Ours is not a faith for nitwits, which
is *not* to say that different people don't have different ca-
pacities of intellect. It's simply to say that every Christian
is expected to think to the best of his or her capacity.

Skepticism is a word that has to do with intellect, not
with attitude. Anyone can be grouchy, but not everyone
can be truly skeptical. Skepticism requires effort, it involves labor; it isn't lazy or sloppy.

A working definition of *skepticism* must go back to the
Greek word from which it is derived, *skeptesthai.* The
word means "to fix one's gaze on," "to look into," "to ex-
amine," "to observe." It has to do with inquiry, consider-
ation, investigation. It isn't synonymous with "doubt," and
it isn't the antithesis of "faith." Richard Dawkins, the out-
spoken evolutionary biologist and critic of religion, for
example, is not so much a "skeptic" as just another atheist with a few provocative arguments in his bag. One can,
of course, be both an atheist and a skeptic, if by "atheism"
one does *not* mean a dogmatic belief in the nonexistence
of deity; but one could just as easily be religious and a
skeptic, or a Christian and a skeptic. Skepticism, again, is
not the same thing as doubt, but rather *the act of looking
hard at things for the purpose of discovering and under-*

standing what may be true about them. Simple denial doesn't qualify any more than simple affirmation.

The key concept here is "truth." Christianity says, of course, that there is such a thing as truth, that it is discoverable, and that there really is an answer to Pilate's notorious question "What is truth?" Skepticism is emphatically not a rejection of the concept of "truth," but a search for it; and it is indeed motivated by the *belief,* or the *faith,* or at least the presentiment, that truth exists. The skeptic is not despairing or cynical, not a malcontent or a curmudgeon. The skeptic may actually prove to be the lone intelligent voice for faith, hope, and love, as well as the other cardinal virtues, long after they've been lost to a jaded, falsely sophisticated, and coarsened culture.

Pilate, as many have commented down the centuries, embodies just such a cultural stance. After he asks Jesus his question, he walks away from him. If he had been a skeptic, he wouldn't have been so dismissive. Apparently Pilate thought he had posed an "unanswerable" question to this hillbilly holy man, one intended to silence a response rather than invite one. So he withdrew. If he had been a skeptic, however, he conceivably might have asked the same question, but he also might have waited around to hear an answer.

The Greek word for "truth" is *aletheia,* and it means

rather more than the opposite of falsehood or error. It can justifiably be translated as "reality," since the word essentially means "not oblivion." In other words, "truth" is that which is "not empty," "not void," "not shadowy," "not vanity"; in other words, it refers to that which is substantial, lasting, enduring, *real*. When Ecclesiastes assigns all things under the sun to the windy and transient, the futile and vain, he is lamenting the absence of the true and firm in his experience.

When Christ, on the other hand, speaks of "truth" in John's Gospel, he is referring to that which will endure when all that is vanity has disappeared for good. Pilate, it might be said, is someone who represents precisely the opposite. He is the spokesman for the transient and empty. He is a representative of the Roman Empire, the dominant and allegedly "eternal" kingdom of his own long-gone, blown-away age. He occupies his small, short-lived place, doubtful of the existence of truth. If he had at least been a skeptic, he would have known that he was ignorant, that human knowledge is puny and severely limited. He might not so quickly have walked away thinking he knew more about reality and life than Jesus.

Skepticism, unlike doubt, looks for truth, but it also perceives that human knowledge alone is inadequate for the task of discovering it. The great lie of the modern world is that "science" can discover the truth through empirical research. No one should deny the value and grandeur revealed since the scientific revolution began, nor make an attempt to contradict the scientific quest with the religious one. But science uncovers facts, not truth. Truth includes the facticity of facts, but transcends mere facts. Facts are fluid, come and gone; truth is greater than the sum of all facts. Philosophy and religion deal with truth; science is not equipped to do this, even if it adds to the philosophical and religious questions that are asked.

But human knowledge at its best knows that it doesn't know; it knows that it can only know what it knows surrounded by a "cloud of unknowing." In fact, it strongly suspects that any human pursuit for what might be real and lasting requires help from outside itself. The doubter immediately concludes that the search is therefore meaningless and futile. He walks away. The skeptic, ever the optimist in the face of such close-mindedness, isn't so sure.

The first thing, then, that a real skeptic is skeptical of is unaided human thought and knowledge. This is absolutely necessary for us to get clear and sharp in our minds if we're going to go any further in our appreciation of skepticism. *Skepticism is firstly self-critical.* The moment I say "I know," I *may* very well have just closed myself off from knowing something as I might more truly know it. "Now that you say, 'We see,' your guilt remains" (John 9:41). "If any one imagines that he knows something, he does not yet know as he ought to know" (1 Cor. 8:2).

TRUTH, whatever it is, will certainly prove complex. Skepticism is recognition of that basic perception. We might wish, in reductionist style, that truth were simple (as the atheists do), that faith was more cut-and-dried than it is (as many believers do); but skeptics know better than that. That's not to say they occasionally are not tempted themselves to wish for "a simpler faith" or a more easily digestible "truth." Human knowledge falters before truth, and must always see its gains as an incomplete grasp of some infinitesimally small portion of it. It must have the humility and maturity to accept ambiguity, gray areas, and paradox. "Sight" may be "blindness," "knowledge" may be "ignorance," a purported "good" may turn out to be a monstrous "evil," a "known fact" may prove "false," and so on. In short, what often is declared to be "simple faith" or "common sense" or "status quo" may turn out to be, in the end, ungodly, untrue, and inhumane. History is replete with examples of blood shed, peoples starved or enslaved or imprisoned, lives trapped and ruined, hopes crushed, innocence violated, dangerous fools in command, goodness unrecognized, and countless other iniquities perpetrated for what appeared at one time or another to be the very best of "simple" and "common" ideas, the wisest of options. Pop atheists of late have laid all this wickedness at the feet of "religion," as if secularism and atheism have nothing to answer for, especially in the bloodiest century (the twentieth) in history to date. This is too easy, as any skeptic would know instantly. The problem is something awry in the human condition, something more bestial than rational; and that "something," whatever one wishes to call it — and it's certainly not "religion" any more than it's science, singing, or art — "poisons everything" (*pace* Christopher Hitchens).

So, a skeptic is not too quick to accept anything at face value. He knows that reason alone "is sure to err." Whatever "it" is, "it" must be examined — and even then one mustn't be too quick to have done with it after an apparent conclusion.

Consequently, a skeptic simply cannot view doubt as a good thing. Doubt can be unhealthy and destructive, and — because it is every bit as fallible a mind-set as gullibility — it's not to be considered a better road to go than faith. At least, "faith seeks understanding"; doubt can't seek anything, it can only doubt. Faith can be good ground for skepticism; doubt can't really be skeptical about anything except, one would wish, itself — and then, of course, it's in danger of believing something after all.

Faith and Skepticism

SKEPTICISM WITHIN the context of Christian belief is, I think, a good thing. It is firmly rooted in a Hebrew concept of faith, one that instinctively distrusts human reason, recognizing its fallibilities and limitations, but embraces relational trust (the true meaning of "faith") in a self-revealing and self-interpreting God. It is a faith open to questioning God, examining his ways, complaining to him, and even expressing exasperation and impatience at his silence. It is a faith that admits sorrow and sadness and mental darkness, one that places melancholy before God in a place of legitimacy, as well as a sense of humor. It allows that anger at God can be expressed without blasphemy, that a man may have honest reason to demand, with Abraham, justice from his Creator: "Shall not the Judge of all the earth do right?" (Gen. 18:25). This question, which "our father in the faith" put to God, runs clear through the Bible. It is echoed in Jesus' cry from the cross. Such a faith embraces the best aspects of conventional piety and yet goes beyond its limitations. In modern jargon, it "thinks outside the box." More to the point, this is the kind of faith we find in the Bible itself.

So, I cursorily present here what a Christian skeptic should perhaps be prepared to avoid intellectually. I go out on a limb here, realizing that such a list — likely an incomplete one — will raise the hackles of not a few of my co-religionists. Yet, I think that such a *via media* is an honest and thoughtful place to be. (Indeed, ever since the demise of Anglicanism in its healthiest form, I have come to think that there is a vital need for the place it once held among the Christian churches — the *via media* of a faithful skepticism, rooted in Scripture, informed by tradition, and reasonable; without fanaticism on the one hand or a fussy rationalism on the other, with cool mind but warm piety.)

The Christian skeptic, then, refuses the following:

A thoughtless Biblicism. He reads the Bible "like any other book," as Benjamin Jowett put it in 1860. In other words, he reads it with critical attention to its various literary genres, its cultural parameters, its canonical shaping by various historical communities, its numerous authors' purposes in writing, and its levels of meaning (literal and "spiritual"). It is "inspired," but in the Hebrew, not the Greek, sense of that attribution, with emphasis put on its overall message and not on some theory of word-by-word transcription. It is God's Word written, as received by faith; but it is a human book nonetheless, and open to scrutiny, and therefore to faithful skepticism. It is "divine and human" in origin; but it isn't to be read as Muslims read the Koran. We believe in "inspiration," not dictation.

A thoughtless dogmatism and traditionalism. No Christian, and no sensible pagan, either, would deny that some things, some beliefs and teachings, whether sacred or secular, must be "dogmatic" in nature. As G. K. Chesterton remarked somewhere, any firmly held belief is dogmatic and creedal in nature — for example, the dogma that my mother was indeed my mother and behaved toward me in motherly fashion. Likewise, we all live lives molded by traditions of all sorts. But, when the dogmas are presented in such a way that they stifle questioning or thinking, or if traditions — ritual, devotional, or customary; Byzantine, Latin, or Reformed — are merely archaic vestiges with no sound reason for their untenable persistence (possibly "rendering null and void the Word of God"), then these rightly come under the searching gaze of the faithful skeptic. If there is any reason in a given dogma or tradition, it can be searched out and known, and no harm will ever come to truth in the process — if indeed it *is* truth.

A thoughtless moralism. Morality and ethics are derived from the character of God himself, so a Christian believes. The Ten Commandments and the Sermon on the Mount, for example, regulate our standards of conduct. But these are tempered by the Gospel's emphasis on grace, that Christ is a Physician and a Shepherd of souls, and that holiness is a divine gift with which we learn over a lifetime to cooperate. We are not under law, but grace, not under condemnation, but the Good News of salvation; and therefore our ethics are not to be those of the legalist, but instead of the healer and transformer. Christianity, despite some rigorist naysayers to the contrary, is *therapeutic* in nature. Confession and forgiveness are medicinal. The skeptic, therefore, turns a critical gaze on anyone too quick with such words as "should" and "ought" and "must" when these are used to guide the moral transformation of others. These are fine words, surely, but can be used rightly only by spiritual *physicians,* not "wannabe" lawyers and judges and ecclesiastical cops. Life is without doubt morally messy, but it's never cleaned up by shouting loudly rules and regulations. Jesus illustrated this very point while eating with sinners.

A thoughtless "liberalism." The so-called religious liberalism of the moment (not of the past) is frequently little more than an increasingly bellicose, legalistic, dogmatic, pugnacious, and unreasonable assault on Judeo-Christian morality. I don't refer here to an intellectually flexible and openly dialogical tradition, which is what was once meant by "liberalism." I mean here the groundless loosening of allegedly restrictive ethical (mainly sexual) principles altogether. If moralism has too often been a plague, its libertine counterpart has proven to be just as — and probably even more — hurtful. Little needs to be said here, except that the faithful skeptic will look at this sham long and hard, and recognize it for the shallow self-justification it is, chalking it up as yet another symptom of latter-day nihilism.

THE CHRISTIAN skeptic, then, walks a fine line. He is not a "fundamentalist" in the popular sense, including the "liberal" variety. He adheres to what is fundamental, which is his faith — his personal trust — in the God who has revealed himself and is himself the truth. Truth, that which is substantial and lasting, is the only foundation he trusts, even if he knows that it is far vaster than his human reason can ever manage or comprehend.

He reads the Bible, prays, worships, and leads a life growing — he hopes — in holiness. But he reads the Bible intelligently (as a "rational sheep"); he says his prayers even when he can't pray (as Georges Bernanos suggested somewhere); he worships, but not as someone wishing to escape, or to be overwhelmed by ornate and misty "mysteries," or drawn into some emotional expression of euphoria or hysteria; he seeks to live a moral life, not a rule-based, law-book one which too easily gives one a false sense of smug security.

The faithful Christian skeptic has, finally, really only one single irreducible standard for his life: Jesus Christ. Here, before whom an uncomprehending Pontius Pilate could only ask his question and walk away, the Christian sees "truth" in human flesh and blood. But, in seeing truth in Jesus, the genuine skeptic must now become ever more committed to looking at and pondering everything else in relation first and foremost to *Him*.

So he keeps his eyes open, and that means he knows — along with love and joy and humor and other pleasant things — the presence of sorrow within. The skeptical Christian cannot ignore the world in which he lives, nor be insensitive to the lives of people around him, nor be ignorant of the darkness within himself. As Jung wrote in the quotation that appears at the front of this book, "Knowing your own darkness is the best method for dealing with the darknesses of other people."

The skeptic examines all things and knows all things to be, in the end, "spiritual" in nature; and that includes all the problems he sees — those within himself and those in the world around him. The faithful skeptic faces God with questions and anxieties and interior discomforts. He recognizes the disparity between his understanding of God and his own perception of the world; and he knows that these things somehow both challenge his faith and yet — mysteriously — explain each other at some just barely intuited level. The skeptical Christian knows that his intellect and perceptions have been crucified with Christ. Even his dark moments of religious disillusionment are related to the cross, and may prove in the end to be the origin of new light for him.

So, the skeptic is almost always a fundamentally melancholy person, although he may simultaneously be a serenely happy person (the two are not necessarily mutually exclusive).

We look next, then, at melancholy and faith.

Chapter Three

Sorrow in the Kingdom of God

The sacrifice acceptable to God is a broken spirit;
a broken and contrite heart, O God, thou wilt
not despise.

PSALM 51 (50):17

For my soul is full of troubles,
and my life draws near to Sheol.
I am reckoned among those who go down
to the Pit;
I am a man who has no strength,
like one forsaken among the dead,
like the slain that lie in the grave,
like those whom thou dost remember no more,
for they are cut off from thy hand.
Thou hast put me in the depths of the Pit,

Sorrow in the Kingdom of God

in the regions dark and deep . . .
But I, O LORD, cry to thee;
in the morning my prayer comes before thee.
O LORD, why dost thou cast me off?
Why dost thou hide thy face from me? . . .
Thou hast caused lover and friend to shun me;
my companions are in darkness.

PSALM 88 (87):3-6, 13-14, 18

For my days pass away like smoke,
and my bones burn like a furnace.
My heart is smitten like grass, and withered;
I forget to eat my bread.
Because of my loud groaning
my bones cleave to my flesh.
I am like a vulture of the wilderness,
like an owl of the waste places;
I lie awake,
I am like a lonely bird on the housetop.
All the day my enemies taunt me,
those who deride me use my name for a curse.
For I eat ashes like bread,
and mingle tears with my drink,
because of thy indignation and anger;
for thou hast taken me up and thrown me away.

KNOWING DARKNESS

My days are like an evening shadow;
  I wither away like grass.

PSALM 102 (101):3-11

I am the man who has seen affliction
  under the rod of his wrath;
he has driven and brought me
  into darkness without any light;
surely against me he turns his hand
  again and again the whole day long.
He has made my flesh and my skin waste away,
  and broken my bones;
he has besieged and enveloped me
  with bitterness and tribulation;
he has made me dwell in darkness
  like the dead of long ago.
He has walled me about so that I cannot escape;
  he has put heavy chains on me;
though I call and cry for help,
  he shuts out my prayer;
he has blocked my way with hewn stones,
  he has made my paths crooked. . . .

LAMENTATIONS 3:1-9

Sorrow in the Kingdom of God

He was despised and rejected by men;
  a man of sorrows, and acquainted with grief;
and as one from whom men hide their faces
  he was despised, and we esteemed him not.
Surely he has borne our griefs
  and carried our sorrows,
yet we esteemed him stricken,
  smitten by God, and afflicted.

ISAIAH 53:3-4

Blessed are those who mourn, for they shall be comforted.

MATTHEW 5:4

Jesus wept.

JOHN 11:35

And when he drew near and saw the city he wept over it. . . .

LUKE 19:41

And he took with him Peter and James and John, and began to be greatly distressed and troubled. And he said to them, "My soul is very sorrowful, even to death. . . ."

MARK 14:33-34

For I wrote you out of much affliction and anguish of heart and with many tears, not to cause you pain but to let you know the abundant love that I have for you.

2 CORINTHIANS 2:4

For even if I made you sorry with my letter, I do not regret it. . . . For godly grief produces a repentance that leads to salvation and brings no regret, but worldly grief produces death.

2 CORINTHIANS 7:8, 10

A S THIS sampling of biblical texts shows, sorrow and grief are to be found among the holiest of persons. The Bible, with its unvarnished picture of human life, its utter lack of sentimentality, its frankness and straightforwardness, never confuses faith with perpetual "happiness" or "living in the victory" or "the joy-filled life" or anything akin to a greeting-card, "Precious Moments" outlook. There is nothing even remotely cozy, in the dreamy Kinkade-cottagey sort of way, to be found there.

For instance, in Psalm 88 (87) above, the Psalmist complains bitterly to God in terms of near despair, even concluding his long lamentation on a note of misery rather than the expected one of vindication. Like the author of the book of Lamentations, or like Job (as we shall see later), he doesn't hesitate to confront God about his afflictions, and the suggestion — or rather, accusation — is that God is not treating him fairly but instead much too roughly.

That this kind of railing against God can be part of true piety seems foreign to some of us, raised as we sometimes were with a residual Victorian fastidiousness about being impolite, especially to or about God. It's "not nice" to cry out to God in anger, to demand answers, to say what we feel from our hearts (even though God can look within us and see much more terrible things than anger and disappointment there). But, if the Bible is a standard, then even such displays of temper and honesty and bitterness in our prayers can — and ought — to be spoken directly to him. He can take it.

The text of Isaiah 53, another example above, is applied to Jesus more than once in the New Testament. It describes "a man of sorrows." The Gospels make clear that indeed Jesus was just such a man. The New Testament message in fact is that when the Messiah came into the world, he "carried our sorrows" — the sorrows of the whole blighted human lot. More than this, instead of revealing some sort of beatific vision or spiritual technique, Jesus taught his followers to look squarely at the miseries of humanity — indeed, to see him right there, in "the least of these," the poor, the naked, the sick, the imprisoned, the persecuted, and so on, and to respond to these in acts of loving care. The Sermon on the Mount is mostly about how to treat rightly other men and women, and many of the parables reveal that our final judgment will be based on the same. Devotion and mysticism, so stressed by a later Hellenized Christianity, are not emphasized by Jesus, but rather privatized and somewhat downplayed. What is meant to be made visible and public is the Christians' manifest love for those who suffer. There are, throughout the New Testament, numerous exhortations to downward — not upward — mobility, whether one thinks of a worldly or a mystical ascent. It is *downward* — that is, to service of others. And *there* one will meet Christ "in the least"; there will be found — at the bottom of the depths of human squalor and pain — "Emmanuel," "God *with us*." The way of Christian discipleship — symbolized by Jesus himself as "carrying the cross" — is to a great extent a sorrowful way because it is walked with eyes wide open to the world in all its adversities and wretchedness.

The Apostle Paul, in imitation of his Master, was likewise a "man of sorrows," and he saw further the occasional need for sorrow within the life of faith as the necessary way to bring his widespread congregations face to face with unpleasant facts about themselves, as the pertinent quotes above make evident. In other words, Christians occasionally, perhaps frequently, have need of sorrow in order to *repent* (the word means "change of mind") of certain behaviors and attitudes that are hypocritical or immoral, so that they can continue to act before the gaze of the world as the followers of Christ should.

IF WE TURN again to look at the sorrow of Christ himself, we find ourselves looking at something close to the heart of our understanding of the nature of God, something of greater significance to us than either the sorrows of the Psalmist or our own personal and communal need to mourn for sin.

To say it simply, it is not so much the *causes* of melancholy in the life of Christ that are most important to us (the death of Lazarus, the plight of Jerusalem, Gethsemane), but rather *who* it is who experienced the sorrow. If Christ was "a man of sorrows," then we must take that very plain assertion about his character seriously indeed. It can't be ignored. We should not forget it in the face of the rather nauseating popularity of kitschy depictions of a laughing Christ and a grinning, blow-dried Jesus. Neither should we associate it with the sentimentalized, dewy-eyed "holy card" images of a sweetly "sorrowful" Jesus, so popular in an earlier age. And, again, we should look past every depiction of Christ we have ever seen on the movie screen, including Mel Gibson's. None of these will ultimately do; they are too close to the merely bathetic, the dramatic or artfully cinematic, or (as in the case of "happy Jesus") somebody's trite wishful thinking.

The sadness of Jesus, more than anything else Christians find in their Scriptures, gives good reason to see melancholy — even if it's recognizably a case of clinical depression — as something that potentially possesses meaning. The One who sees all things as they truly are, clearly and perfectly, in whom the fullness of the Godhead dwells bodily, *also wept.* He also said, "My soul is very sorrowful, *even to death*." This is — let us be clear on the point — Jesus saying that he feels as if he could end it all here and now, that he could die in his depression.

The sorrow of Christ has nothing to do with personal repentance, still less with anger at God. Since we believe that Jesus is "God with us," we identify his sorrow as something that expresses the divine mind as well as his human nature. In fact, in every human action of Christ, the Christian is meant to see the divine simultaneously, since what we know of God can most definitively be known through the terms of Christ's real and fleshly humanity.

What, in fact, Jesus revealed in that humanity — as "God with us" — was the enormous truth that "God is love." First John 4:8b-10 says it this way: "... God is love. In this the love of God was made manifest among us, that God sent his only Son into the world, so that we might live through him. In this is love, not that we loved God but that he loved us and sent his Son to be the expiation for our sins." St. Paul puts it like this in Romans 5:8: "But God shows his love for us in that while we were yet sinners Christ died for us." This is hardly a syrupy, sentimental sort of revelation, since undergoing cruel death for others' sakes is not exactly the stuff of fluffy sentimentalism. No "Precious Moments" here. Nor is the statement that "God is love" an ontological or philosophical one about "hypostatic" relations within the Trinity, as has been sometimes asserted by theologians. That's a fine idea, certainly, but it belongs to a more Greek mode of abstract thinking about "essence" and "being" and "deity." No, this Jewish-Christian claim has to do with God's outpouring of love on human beings, seen most austerely in the cross of Jesus.

SIMILARLY, when the Scriptures make use of such striking language as "the Kingdom of God" and "the *Logos* ["Message"] made flesh" and "the Light shining in the darkness," all such phrases are impossible of interpretation and could be — and have been — meat for mere philosophical abstraction (and therefore useless), when set apart from the actions and words of Jesus in the Gospels. The Bible knows nothing of Scholasticism, that theological so-called science that exists to slice the baloney ever thinner. Rather, such phrases refer to what cannot adequately be articulated at all, philosophically or otherwise, and — since all language is essentially metaphorical, even in what we consider to be common and "straightforward" parlance — they point to what is to be *experientially* known or *lived out in relation* to God.

To make a comparison, someone has said that trying to explain with precision the Chinese word *Tao* is virtually impossible, even to the Chinese themselves. That's because the *Tao* is something to be lived, not to be talked about (as the classic *Tao Te Ching* says right at its beginning, for example). It is a "way" of life, the meaning of which can only be found in "following" it.

In the New Testament, this way of using language to suggest what ultimately cannot be articulated is precisely how Jesus uses the metaphor of "the Kingdom of God." Jesus wasn't saying that God's *basileia* ("Kingdom" = "empire") was like the Roman *basileia,* which is precisely the pervasive, world-dominating entity of his own historical experience to which he was making a sharp contrast. "*My* kingship," he tells Pilate, just before the subject of "Truth" is brought up, "is *not* of this world; *if* my kingship were of this world, *my servants would fight . . .*" (John 18:36; italics mine). In other words, Christ's (God's)

Kingdom is not like the Roman one — not militaristic, not hierarchical in its structure, not run by so-called benefactors who lord it over others (cf. Mark 10:42-44 and similar passages).

Jesus very rarely uses hierarchical or "empire" language to describe the Kingdom he announces; and on those few occasions when he does, he only refers to a "king" or a rich "owner" who represents God or the Son of Man, and no mere worldly person. Mostly, though, he holds up slaves, servants, children, shepherds, and so on as models for those who really should possess influence in his "empire" — none of these social categories possessing any influence, prestige, or "rule" in the ancient (and, indeed, modern) world.

Jesus speaks not in terms of "leadership" but in terms of service. Ambition is out; political power-wielding is out; acquisition of wealth and status is out. He establishes his "Kingdom" as, in concept, *the very antithesis of the Roman kingdom.* The "joke," if I may call it that, is that God's "Kingdom" is, in the eyes of the world, an "un-kingdom"; but, in the eyes of God, all the kingdoms of the earth are dust on the scales and drops in the bucket.

"The Kingdom of God," as Jesus uses the term, is intentionally a radical, undermining, subversive presence that upsets the world's ideas of authority and influence. He uses the word *basileia* in an ironical fashion. It's here, present, growing right under the noses of the earthly powers. It can't be stopped, and in God's good time it will be fully realized.

St. Paul clearly understood the meaning of Jesus, describing God's *basileia* in terms of the *sort of life* Christians were meant to be living (similar, in some interesting respects, to the idea of living according to the *Tao,* as presented by the early Taoist sages): "The kingdom of God *is* . . . righteousness and peace and joy in the Holy Spirit [Breath]" (Rom. 14:17). Since that is what it *is,* then any notion that the "Kingdom of God" is merely to be identified with an institutional church, for instance, cannot be sustained, and cannot be sustained anywhere else in the New Testament.

The reason this term historically becomes misunderstood is due to the fact that, when the Roman Empire became "Christianized," it failed to recognize the implicit irony of Jesus' appropriation of the term. Jesus had utilized the word *basileia* precisely to turn the concept upside down and pull it inside out. From the time of Constantine on, however, there was to be, absurdly and grimly, a "Christian" emperor, a "Christian" military, a "Christian" political system, and so on. There was to be, as well, a "Christian" ecclesiastical "hierarchy" — problematic, in light of the directives of Jesus himself, who said nothing about establishing a "*rule* of priests," but instead taught "priestly" *service* exercised with the humility and accountability expected of mere stewards.

Forgotten, with the emergence of "Christendom," was Christ's original meaning of "the Kingdom of God" in all its ironic purity. The implicit humor was lost, the severely intentional contrast smeared and washed out into gray. The "Kingdom" as a "way of living" was compromised; and instead there returned an older, stern, worldly, "Roman" understanding of external, overbearing, law-brandishing "empire." And this was ossified into an often oppressive and deadly serious political and institutional system. "Kingdom of God," in other words, was in turn appropriated, inverted, objectified, hardened, and misinterpreted in the Byzantine East, the Latin West, and later the Reformed West with its "national" churches. Mostly it was not done cynically or consciously; it was not a "plot" or a conspiracy. Still, as Malcolm Muggeridge put it in one of his writings, ever since Jesus said that his Kingdom was not of this world, people — sadly, Christians — have tried to prove him wrong.

But the point here really is this: To see "the Kingdom" most clearly represented, one has to look to the person of Jesus — his "way" of life, what he taught, the "orthopraxy" he demanded of his followers, his nonviolence, and so much else. The lesson to be learned is that we are not free to decide, as post-Constantinian Christendom tended to do, what the word *Kingdom* means and then apply *our own* notions to Jesus' use of the term. Instead, we interpret what he meant by looking and listening only to him.

And, for Jesus, the Kingdom of God is seen when his followers see suffering human beings and serve them. It is seen at the lowest point, where God himself descended in Christ — into the depths of despair, futility, death, and every human ill. For all the implicit irony in the term, the "Kingdom" that God establishes is intended to show Christ-like sorrow in the face of appalling realities and convert it into actions of love toward our neighbors. Here is the authentically Christian enlightenment to be found; here is the real mysticism of the cross: in the words of Blessed Teresa of Calcutta, here is "Christ in his distressing disguise."

RETURNING, THEN, to the Christian concept of *love* and the statement that "*God* is love," we similarly find in it something that cannot be grasped apart from looking at Jesus himself. Apart from him, this truth about God would be unknowable in any distinct way. In fact, going back to the idea of foundational "Truth" in the last chapter, "God is love" is the very essence of that Truth. It is the content of Truth, as Christians have it. Here, then, is an infinitely deep revelation, and no matter how deeply one delves into the nature of all things — the myriad aspects of existence, the multitudinous thoughts of the human heart, and finally the unique mystery of the cross — what the Christian means by "love" is there and lies even further beyond still, always permeating but always ungraspable. It upholds and contains all things, but is itself contained by nothing; and therefore it *is* God — God *is* love. What Jesus does in his person is to *demonstrate* it.

The sadness, the sorrow, the melancholy of Jesus reveals something, both about the Kingdom of God that awaits its fullest realization in a renewed creation, and about the nature of the love of God. Christ's sorrow is, therefore, itself *revelation,* and related intimately to his divine self-emptying (cf. Phil. 2:5-11; John 13:1-20).

In Luke's Gospel, Jesus' rejoicing has to do with his elation that what he has come to reveal has been received by the childlike in heart: "In that same hour he rejoiced in the Holy Spirit and said, 'I thank thee, Father, Lord of heaven and earth, that thou hast hidden these things from the wise and understanding and revealed them to babes; yea, Father, for such was thy gracious will'" (Luke 10:21). Likewise, his later sorrow has to do with the fact that what he has come to reveal has been rejected in Jerusalem: "And when he drew near and saw the city he wept over it, saying, 'Would that even today you knew the things that make for peace! But now they are hid from your eyes'" (Luke 19:41-42). Jesus displays both joy and sorrow in relation to how his revelation of God is received.

In Mark and Matthew we find poignant descriptions of Christ's sorrow in Gethsemane: "And he took with him Peter and James and John, and began to be greatly distressed and troubled. And he said to them, 'My soul is very sorrowful, even to death . . .'" (Mark 14:33-34; cf. Matt. 26:37-38). (It is worth noting in passing that Jesus, in his distress, turns to his three closest friends for company, although they prove unable to meet the challenge on this terrible occasion. It's a striking reminder of the high premium he placed on friendship, a memory of his character stressed most particularly in John's Gospel. We will come back to this in a later chapter.) What is revealed here is the full extent of God's love in Christ: utter self-giving for others in the face of suffering and annihilation. "Greater love has no man than this, that a man lay down his life for his friends" (John 15:13).

It is strikingly in the context of the death of a friend, Lazarus, that Jesus displays sadness in John's Gospel. The Bible's shortest verse, John 11:35, reads simply, "Jesus wept." His public expression of emotion is commented on (accurately) by some of the onlookers: "See how he loved him!" (John 11:36). What follows is the raising of Lazarus from the dust of the grave, a scene that recalls the forming of the first man from the dust of the ground (Gen. 2:7).

Jesus weeps; his sorrow is related to love; his love raises a man to life, signifying the greater promise of a new creation; and all this is done — as Jesus declares openly — to *reveal* what God is doing in Christ: "I have said this on account of the people standing by, that they may believe that thou [the Father] didst send me" (John 11:42).

As with "Kingdom" and "love," we want to avoid any rigid definitions of "melancholy" or "sorrow" in Jesus' case. We want only to suggest some connections, which are connections between love and revelation and sorrows. Jesus' sorrows are involved in the sorrows of a "fallen" creation and humanity, into which he has entered through his self-emptying of divine status. The term *fallen* may be better understood in the modern context if we replace this word with *incomplete* or *unfulfilled*. Something — evil, sin — has retarded the movement of creation toward its intended end; and man has not become — as also intended — the perfect image of God. St. Paul describes this earthly condition in these terms:

> I consider that the sufferings of this present time are not worth comparing with the glory that is to be revealed in us. For the creation waits with eager longing for the revealing of the sons of God; for the creation was subjected to futility, not of its own will but by the will of him who subjected it in hope; be-

cause the creation itself will be set free from its bondage to decay and obtain the glorious liberty of the children of God. We know that the whole creation has been groaning in travail together until now; and not only the creation, but we ourselves, who have the first fruits of the Spirit, groan inwardly as we wait for adoption as sons, the redemption of our bodies. For in this hope we were saved.... (Rom. 8:18-24a)

"Groaning" and "hope" are tied together; human destiny and the future of the creation are inextricably one. We "who have the first fruits of the Spirit" still participate in the "futility" of "this present time": we still suffer, become ill, face unpredictable disasters and terrible debilitations, lose our loved ones, have our lives disrupted by others' evil, encounter injustices, grow old and perish. This is what is meant by "the whole creation groaning in travail"; and we followers of Christ "groan" with it. Into this semi-chaotic, still half-baked, unfinished order, "subjected to futility," Jesus came, and there planted the Kingdom of God and revealed the God who is love. Where there should be only hopelessness, Christ reveals hope. His resurrection sows the seed which promises that "the creation itself will be set free from its bondage to decay and obtain the glorious liberty of the children [those in the process of growing into the image] of God." Creation sorrows, we sorrow, and the sorrows of Christ show God embracing and taking up these sorrows; and, by so doing, God offers hope beyond all our sorrows.

The melancholy of Jesus intersects with the sorrows we all experience ourselves. It is related to our own "groanings" in this life. "For we have not a high priest who is unable to sympathize with our weaknesses" (Heb. 4:15a). It reveals that "God is love," and it underscores that his "Kingdom" is not of this world — neither a triumphalistic ecclesiastical institution nor the religious wing of some power-brokering secular government. Christ's earthly sorrows — now transcended by the infinite joy of his exaltation — once reflected the situation of "this present time," and they were the divine response of "the Resurrection and the Life" to futility and death.

All our sorrows and sadnesses are originally related to the sense of futility and knowledge of the fact of death (only human beings can sense and know these things and feel their immense weight on the mind), and a skeptic will see these things for what they are and lament them. But the message of Jesus, in the face of such enveloping darkness, is nonetheless "Blessed are those who mourn, for they shall be comforted." Our "groaning" is justified. We don't need to feel ashamed of having a faith that must occasionally be marked by melancholy, so long as we also hold on to the message of the Kingdom and the hope held out to us by Jesus. In turn, sorrow finds its true value when it moves us to love and the service of others.

If we do these things, we will also know something of "the righteousness and peace and joy in the Holy Spirit," *which is* the Kingdom of God — things we might not see so vividly or savor so well if we didn't also know something of the darkness of futility and death, realms not alien to God.

Chapter Four

The Bible's Kerouac:
Ecclesiastes

I F SEPTEMBER 5, 2007, marked the tenth anniversary of the death of Mother Teresa with the publication of her private letters and journals, that same month, day, and year marked the fiftieth anniversary of another, very different sort of publication. On September 5, 1957, *On the Road* burst onto the literary scene, the quintessential statement in novel form of the "Beat Generation." Its author, and the man who coined the elusive and oblique term "Beat" (as in "beatific vision," "I feel dead 'beat,'" and "the beat goes on"), was Jack Kerouac, a native of the Massachusetts mill town of Lowell. Since its initial publication, the book has never gone out of print, and it still sells approximately a whopping hundred thousand copies a year.

On the Road is a fictionalized account of Kerouac's

several jaunts back and forth from coast to coast and down into Mexico with his friend Neal Cassady (renamed Dean Moriarty in the novel) and others. In its pages can be found pseudonymous thumbnail portraits of other influential Beats like William Burroughs and Allen Ginsberg. It's a rambling, wild, picaresque book, its verbal cadences and rhythms influenced by the jazz Kerouac loved. It celebrates a breaking free from the oppressive buttoned-down boredom of post–World War II society, with its stifling trivialities and fake optimism, so strikingly at odds with the psychological and ethical trauma that the invention and use of the atom bomb had created; and it is the expression of a quest for living life directly before (as everyone feared) life as we know it might get snuffed out permanently. Kerouac straightforwardly tells about his adventures, including his indulgence in drugs, drink, and sex. To find firsthand an involvement with sheer existence, he launched himself with urgency and even a wacky kind of innocence into everything he could experience for himself. And so, without ever intending it, Kerouac helped father the counterculture that was to follow and then flourish over the next decade and a half.

But — surprising perhaps to those with only superficial acquaintance with his work — Jack Kerouac was horrified by this charge being laid at his door. One of his last essays was entitled "After Me, the Deluge," which first appeared in 1969 in the September 28 issue of *The Chicago Tribune.* There he soundly rejected the revolutionaries of the Sixties. "I'm not a Tax-Free, not a Hippie-Yippie — I must be a Bippie-in-the-middle," he asserted. "No, I'd better go around and tell everybody, or let others convince me, that I'm the great white father and intellectual forebear who spawned a deluge of alienated radicals, war protesters, dropouts, hippies and even 'beats.'"[1] Unlike his friend Allen Ginsberg, who jumped right from San Francisco "beat" to San Francisco hippie, Kerouac had little patience with "hippie flower children out in the park with their peanut butter sandwiches and their live-and-let-live philosophy."[2] He even claimed to espouse the conservatism exemplified by William F. Buckley Jr.

Be that as it may, Kerouac, experimenting in both wisdom and folly in his numerous cross-country ramblings, was nevertheless a deeply religious man, and his searching was of the spiritual kind. This can be glimpsed already when, early in *On the Road,* he wrote, "The only people for me are the mad ones, the ones who are mad to live, mad to talk, mad to be saved, desirous of everything

1. Jack Kerouac, "After Me, the Deluge," in *The Portable Kerouac* (New York: Penguin Books, 1996), pp. 573ff.

2. Jack Kerouac, "After Me, the Deluge," pp. 573ff.

at the same time, the ones who never yawn or say a commonplace thing, but burn, burn, burn like fabulous yellow Roman candles exploding like spiders across the stars and in the middle you see the blue centerlight pop and everybody goes 'Aww!'"[3] The spiritual element becomes even more obvious in *The Dharma Bums,* the book he wrote immediately after *On the Road.* Here we read of his pursuit of truth in Buddhism, and there is a sort of purity of heart (which is, as Kierkegaard put it, "to will one thing") in this book even when there is some confusion of mind in working through his superabundance of impressions. Still, *The Dharma Bums* is a book that reaches its conclusion with Kerouac up on Desolation Peak in Washington state, after living alone in a shack there for months, saying, "God, I love you . . . I have fallen in love with you, God. Take care of us all, one way or the other."[4]

Kerouac died in 1969 at the age of forty-seven. He drank himself to death, melancholic, depressed, burnt out. He also died, as paradoxically as he lived, a convinced Catholic, having returned to the faith of his childhood. Not a liberal, not really a conservative, certainly a loner, but a Catholic with a deep devotion to the cross.

3. Jack Kerouac, *On the Road* (New York: Penguin Essential Editions, 2005), Part 1, chap. 1, pp. 5-6.

4. Jack Kerouac, *The Dharma Bums* (New York: Penguin Books, 1976), chap. 34, p. 244.

The sufferings of Jesus could visibly move him to tears. When asked once why he didn't commit suicide, the response was typical of him: he said he was a Catholic, and so he couldn't kill himself. Yet, sadly, he did precisely that, dying of cirrhosis of the liver, in an alcoholic haze. He had long struggled with his alcoholism, as one can see starkly, for instance, in his book *Big Sur.* Although some clever pop-atheist might try to argue otherwise, his faith didn't drive him to such an end; rather, it was his faith that gave him his only real anchor and steadied him in his final years. Despite all his interest in Buddhism, it was Jesus that he met in the lowest place, and he died loving Christ and meditating on his sufferings.

Jack Kerouac was the sort of mixture of spirituality and carnality, wisdom and folly, humor and heartbreak, and skepticism and melancholy that one might assume stands very far away from the piety of the Bible. In fact, though, Kerouac's experimentation, personal struggles, and rambling mind and prose remind me of at least one book of the Bible — the book of Ecclesiastes. There we find some of the very same elements, the same sort of wild thinking and experimentation, and indeed the same sort of final weariness and faith intermingled. Kerouac himself made a similar connection between himself and this particular biblical book, as one can see in the very title of his last "novel," *The Vanity of Duluoz,* in which he directly quotes form it. Like Kerouac at the end of his life, Ecclesiastes does not espouse a dissolute lifestyle; his book is a resounding warning against embracing whatever is futile. Similarly, Kerouac later felt — even in the declining days of his rapid "decay" (his word) — that he must protest his lionization by "hippie" nihilists.

A singular enormous difference is to be highlighted in a comparison of these two far-flung figures, however, although of course there are many more differences much too obvious to mention. But the one major difference I wish to point out is that, while Ecclesiastes is the work of a man who had matured and emerged from his years of experimentation with wisdom to convey to others as a teacher, Kerouac never gave himself that chance. Though he clung to the cross, his death nevertheless serves as a dark illustration: it silently demonstrates the very futility that Ecclesiastes decries. What might Kerouac have become if he had emerged from his tunnel instead of dying there, had continued to write and develop his art and thought, as Ecclesiastes evidently did?

On a positive note, however, a younger Kerouac had called himself a "Dharma Bum." Maybe, with a great deal of license, one can picture a young Ecclesiastes — or, Qoheleth — as a "Torah Bum," someone searching for the spirit of the Torah in the experiments and experiences of his own life.

As MENTIONED in the first chapter, I am using the old-fashioned word *melancholy* (from the Greek for "black bile") in its later, developed sense of "a feeling of thoughtful sadness." I don't want to quibble over whether or not this or that particular person's "melancholy" qualifies as an "illness" in clinical contexts; I do want to stress, however, that melancholy is a universal and valid emotion. It is *"thoughtful* sadness."

The Bible's great exemplar of thoughtful sadness is "Qoheleth," or "Ecclesiastes." That this book appears at all in the canon of sacred Scripture is, on the surface of things, surprising, to say the very least. After all, we find voiced here ideas and opinions startlingly at odds with other portions of the Bible. There's something untamable, unpredictable, unsettled and unsettling about Ecclesiastes, just as there is in Jack Kerouac's work. The book intentionally disrupts established pieties, challenges neat cause-and-effect assumptions in areas of morality, and presents God in ways that leave the reader more often than not with questions instead of answers (a trait in common with the book of Job, as we will see). Throughout the book there is a sense of world-weariness, sadness mixed with resignation and sly humor; in fact, it is a thoroughly melancholy and skeptical book.

Little can be ascertained about the author of Ecclesiastes. The book seems to date to the fourth or third century B.C., and certainly is not a product of the period of Solomon, despite the traditional attribution in Ecclesiastes 1:1 ("the son of David, king in Jerusalem") and 1:12. It was commonplace to connect Solomon to "wisdom" literature. (One notable exception, apart from Job, is the book of Sirach, which even goes so far as to call Solomon to task for his foolishness in later life. See Sirach 47:20-21.)

The title "Qoheleth," related to the Hebrew word *qahal* ("assembly" or "congregation"; in Greek, *ekklesia,* from whence derives "Ecclesiastes"), means "a convener of an assembly" or "a gatherer of a congregation." It was rendered in older English translations as "the Preacher," and it seems to be the case that the writer was also a teacher of some note. At least his admiring disciple and editor believed he was. In a concluding addition to the text, this second "wise man" writes of his master, "Besides being wise, Qoheleth also taught the people knowledge, weighing and studying and arranging proverbs with great care. Qoheleth sought to find pleasing words, and uprightly he wrote words of truth" (12:9-10).

So, what sort of "wisdom" and what sort of "truth" confront us in Ecclesiastes? The answer, as already indicated, is the sort of "wisdom" and "truth" that can be born only in "thoughtful sadness." Although it appears that the book is primarily addressed to the young (see, e.g., 9:7-12; 11:9), it is the voice of experience that speaks. It reflects a life that has passed through many contradictions, disillusionments, and disappointments, and which has tasted and tested everything. Having embraced the extremes of wisdom and "madness," it advises neither, but rather a *via media* that accepts life, love, and the ordinary. It counsels both the search for happiness and the fear of God. It enjoins enjoyment "under the sun" of God's material gifts, and reminds the reader of God's judgment as well. There is nothing systematic in these pages. It is existential and humanistic in the best sense of those terms. It confuses us precisely because it shows us life as lived: no neat answers — in fact, more questions than answers — and a growing awareness that for life to be lived as fully as possible in this world, it must avoid both moral dissolution on the one hand and irrational piousness on the other.

Again, it is the editorial hand at the conclusion of the book that gives some helpful overall shape to this accumulation of experiential wisdom: "The sayings of the wise are like goads, and like nails firmly fixed are the collected sayings which are given by one Shepherd [meaning Qoheleth]" (v. 11). Then there is a cautionary word about the fruitlessness of too much study, as if some great search for "life's meaning" through reading many books will actually result in gaining true wisdom (it won't): "My son, beware of anything beyond these

["these" meaning the meager collected sayings of the Shepherd, Qoheleth]. Of making many books there is no end [or, "Making many books serves no purpose" or "Book-learning is a task without end"], and much study is a weariness of the flesh" (v. 12). And then comes the final caution, which in effect says that, although wisdom is learned through life's experiences, as amply evidenced by the sayings of Qoheleth, one still should keep God in view to live one's life sensibly: "The end of the matter; all has been heard. Fear God, and keep his commandments; for this is the whole existence of man. For God will bring every deed into judgment, with every secret thing, whether good or evil" (vv. 13-14). This final exhortation is not merely an "orthodox" corrective to an otherwise "unorthodox" work. Rather, it is somewhat akin to St. Augustine's zen-like dictum "Love God, and do what you will," although one suspects that the more likely sentiment in the spirit of Ecclesiastes would be "*Fear* God, and do what you will." However phrased, it is sound advice, neither dismissive of living out the full — often troubling — experiences of our human lives, nor advocating an overbearing religiousness to stifle ourselves with. There is far more existential freedom implied in this editorial summary than might at first glance be apparent, and Qoheleth, at the conclusion, is shown to have been something of a "Torah Bum."

There is little autobiography by Qoheleth in his book, despite the rather personal confessions of his experiments in life. One passage, though, is tantalizing, and perhaps suggests a lingering sadness in his life that — because of the sheer bitterness of its expression — causes me to wonder if this isn't at least one key to both his melancholy and his skepticism. It comes in 7:25-28:

> I turned my heart [not "mind," as in some translations] to know and to search out and to seek wisdom and the sum of things, and to know the wickedness of folly and the foolishness which is madness. And I found more bitter than death the woman whose heart is snares and nets, and whose hands are fetters; he who pleases God escapes her, but the sinner is taken by her. Behold, this is what I found, says Qoheleth, adding one thing to another to find the sum, which my mind has sought repeatedly, but I have not found. One man among a thousand I found, but a woman among all these I have not found.

Assuming this refers to a personal experience in his life, it suggests a profound loneliness. Some commentators have suggested that this is a general warning against the allurements of a seductress as, for example, is to be found in Proverbs 7:6-27. I find this interpretation unconvincing, and agree with those commentators who find here a warning, engendered by the wise man's own painful experience, cautioning wisdom in affairs of the heart. The analogous verses in Proverbs would then be such grouchy statements as "A wife's quarreling is a continual dripping of rain" (Prov. 19:13b), and "It is better to live in a corner of the housetop than in a house shared with a contentious woman" (Prov. 21:9).

Nonetheless, Qoheleth's complaint is not "sexist," not simply an old curmudgeon's misogynistic sentiment. A woman in circumstances similar to his, but reversed, might conceivably have written, "I found more bitter than death the *man* whose heart is snares and nets," and "*She* who pleases God escapes *him*," and "One *woman* among a thousand I found, but a *man* among all these I have not found." This isn't "gender bias"; rather, it's a poignant statement that expresses one of life's greatest disappointments.

We have no idea, of course, what the moral background is here; or if there was a marriage involved, or simply a liaison of some sort. Perhaps Qoheleth doesn't speak from his own experience at all; but, given the wide range of his life's experiences as he himself enumerates them, it's a good guess that he is drawing upon his own. To this reader it appears, at any rate, that love has eluded him; the love he thought he had found proved in time to be bitter and oppressive. Instead of a companion or "helpmeet," he found emotional deprivation. Although, ideally speaking, "it is not good for the man to be alone," one suspects that Qoheleth may have preferred even the condition of loneliness to the one in which he found himself. Loneliness is a dull, melancholic interior pain, and one can guess that many of the more acerbic sentiments expressed by Qoheleth find their emotional origin here.

Qoheleth not only experienced conjugal frustrations; it's also possible that friendship was difficult for him, given his intelligent, experimenting, and intense personality. Not only was *no woman* temperamentally suited to him, but — for someone of Qoheleth's questing intellect — in the commonality necessary for friendship only "*one man* among a thousand" he found. This growl is really the lamentation for one's sense of intellectual and emotional social isolation. That Qoheleth placed a very high value on friendship is suggested by his sayings on the subject in the fourth chapter: "Two are better than one, because they have a good reward for their toil. For if they fall, one will lift up his fellow; but woe to him who is alone when he falls and has not another to lift him up. Again, if two lie together, they are warm; but how can one be warm alone? And though a man might prevail against one who is alone, two will withstand him. A threefold cord is not quickly broken" (4:9-12).

Perhaps all this is to read too much into the text unnecessarily, but I believe it rings true on a psychological level. One can easily imagine this same man, alone though venerated, a teacher of others but at the same time intellectually unsure in so many things, full of memories of a multitude of experiences good and bad, deeply sensitive to injustice and yet personally deprived emotionally, writing such words as these to a presumably younger audience:

> It is better to go to the house of mourning than to go to the house of feasting; for this is the end of all men, and the living will lay it to heart. Sorrow is better than laughter, for by sadness of countenance the heart is made glad. The heart of the wise is in the house of mourning; but the heart of fools is in the house of mirth. . . . Consider the work of God; who can make straight what he has made crooked? In the day of prosperity be joyful, and in the day of adversity consider; God has made the one as well as the other, so that man may not find out anything that will be after him. . . . Surely there is not a righteous man on earth who does good and never sins. (7:2-4, 13-14, 20)

This might have been similar to the sentiments Jack Kerouac felt at the end of his life toward those young people who thought themselves followers in his footsteps.

Qoheleth's words are brooding ones of resignation and sorrow. They express a skepticism rooted in a lonesome existence. Resignation before the vicissitudes and contradictions of "everything under the sun" is one of the characteristics of Ecclesiastes, an attitude which permeates the whole book. Is it too much to suppose that Qoheleth's personal "quiet desperation" in the matter of love and friendship, his eventual resignation in his private circumstances, led to his larger philosophical resignation in the face of the cosmic *perpetuum mobile* (see 1:3-11; 3:1-9)?

WHATEVER may be conjectured along these lines, it is without doubt the case that Ecclesiastes stands out in the canon of Scripture. Despite the tendency toward philosophical resignation, it isn't an utterly passive mind that is reflected here. Qoheleth hasn't just given up. His book has a tough, individualistic flavor, an audacious uniqueness of vision, reflecting the mind of a genuine, unfettered freethinker — even if the man himself lacked sufficient freedom in other areas of life. For sheer theological daring, not to say cheek, only the book of Job compares. The more fatuous conventions of publicly acceptable piety are not spared his critical scrutiny. The book veers this way and that, contradicts itself, counsels indulgence in the good material and sensual pleasures of life and (as already noted) warns of God's judgment. It denounces injustice, decadence, and every human foible — including the foible of too much religiosity. Something distinctively personal shaped this man, this author of the Bible's most blatantly skeptical book. As noted, it seems reasonable to me that such an individualistic, melancholic view of existence would have been formed in the circumstances of a troubled life, and it is the anxieties surrounding love and personal acceptance that seem to me the likeliest psychological influence on his thought.

Ecclesiastes is also an agnostic book. It doesn't pretend to offer answers; instead, it takes on the most essential questions of life, which is evidenced by the fact that it doesn't superficially seek to reconcile irreconcilable contradictions. It doesn't question the existence of God, certainly, but — for example — it also has no clear view of a life beyond this one, even going so far as to compare the death of human beings to the death of beasts (3:18-21).

There is nothing in the book to suggest that the author thought himself to be conveying revelation. It's an irony — and one supposes Qoheleth himself would have thought so — that this book was ultimately accorded the status of revelation. As revelation, however, it is incomplete; and as a philosophical work, it is even consciously incomplete. It reveals the conundrums of the human condition. It probes the inequities, the acedia, the boredom and weariness, "the sickness unto death," the sense of meaninglessness and purposelessness that haunts the best minds, the madness and follies of "everything under the sun," and it begins and ends (in the original text) with this declaration: "Vanity of vanities, all is vanity" (1:2; 12:8). This is a conclusion that is not a conclusion, a revelation that is open-ended and awaiting fuller revelation.

In Hebrew, the word *vanity* is *hevel,* which means "breath," "vapor," or "mist." It refers to that which is insubstantial, ephemeral, transient, passing away into oblivion. The Septuagint renders the word in Greek as *mataiotes,* meaning "futility," "purposelessness," and "emptiness." Not surprisingly, this is the same word that Paul uses in Romans 8:20, where he writes, "For the creation was subjected to futility [*mataioteti*], not of its own will but by the will of him who subjected it in hope" (see Chapter Two above). Conceptually, too, it stands in stark contrast to the word *truth,* in Greek rendered *aletheia,* which in turn literally means "not oblivion" (see Chapter One above).

Ecclesiastes shows its incompleteness as revelation by proclaiming the insubstantiality of all earthly things: everything will finally pass away like a mist. This is a point repeated in the New Testament: "For the form of this world is passing away" (1 Cor. 7:31b); "And the world passes away" (1 John 2:17a). So, here we have a revelation that is stubbornly humanistic, emanating from a grieving heart and an agnostic mind.

If it is "God's word," it is God's word reaching down and affirming the least religious standpoint of the human soul. Qoheleth, sorrowful, sensitive, acerbic, pained, and lonely, acquired through his troubled reflections the skeptical acuity necessary to challenge conventional piety. That the book became canonical should reveal that conventional piety in fact *needs* to be challenged. Conventional piety — as Jesus himself was to suggest when he referred to the results of pouring new wine into old wineskins or patching old cloth with new, and demonstrated by his severe denunciations of the Sadducees and Pharisees — is not the vehicle for God's most vital action. So it is, in its weariness before the *perpetuum mobile* and its rejection of glib and facile religion, that Ecclesiastes is a *praeparatio evangelica* — a preparing of souls for the radical good news of the Kingdom of God. In its recognition of the insubstantiality of all earthly things, it begs the question implicitly of what God could provide "under the sun" that would prove of substantial, lasting worth. What God in fact did ultimately provide was something so jolting, unexpected, and fundamentally irreligious that even Qoheleth could not have expected it: "We preach Christ crucified, a stumbling block to Jews and folly to Gentiles, but to those who are called, both Jews and Greeks, Christ the power of God and the wisdom of God. For the foolishness of God is wiser than men, and the weakness of God is stronger than men" (1 Cor. 1:23-25).

The message of the cross is certainly not conventional piety. It's a sheer rejection of it, exploding it as surely as new wine would explode old wineskins. The cross as the place where God manifests his glory (John's Gospel in particular emphasizes this) is a shock, an interruption of both religion and the endlessly repeated cycle of history.

Here is the one thing that Qoheleth could most definitely *not* say is "not new under the sun" (1:9). "Is there a thing," he had asked, "of which it is said, 'See, this is new'?" His response: "It has been already, in the ages before us" (1:10). As true as this assertion may be of everything else, it is *not true* of the death and resurrection of Christ, the Word made flesh. The *perpetuum mobile* grinds to a halt; the recurring cycle of times for this and that is shattered; the everlasting Kingdom unexpectedly breaks into a weary world that is passing away. If there is anything akin to *karma* in this world, it's broken by the grace of God. The cross of Christ is especially shocking because it's not a religious answer at all, but a divine answer that is luridly profane in nature. An instrument of torture and capital punishment, reserved for slaves and the dregs of Roman society, becomes the means of salvation right here "under the sun" — and in fact the sun itself is darkened by it. Everything about the cross encompasses and indeed surpasses all the contradictions of wisdom and folly enumerated by Qoheleth. "Has not God made foolish the wisdom of the world?" (1 Cor. 1:20c).

At the end of his life, this was the message of hope in his darkness that Jack Kerouac held onto, his constant devotion at the last, his true *satori.* At the end of Ecclesiastes, this is the one sure answer to the conundrums his book raises about the grinding, circling, sinful, sorrowful continuity of human existence.

So, WHAT IS the sum of all this (as Qoheleth might say)? Simply this: A lonely, melancholic wise man, someone with difficulties in love and friendship — though one suspects he had a large and sensitive soul — a skeptic in the best sense, someone who probably would have been surprised to learn that his rambling text of profane contradictions and sour notes would one day be considered "inspired" as God's own word; this strange convener of the assembly, this curious and troubled Shepherd of disciples, this biblical Kerouac, Qoheleth or Ecclesiastes, is someone whose very profanity points to the Gospel and its unimaginable Sign of Contradiction. Without his melancholy, his loneliness, his skeptical growls and rumblings, we would lack one of the most sophisticated texts of the Old Testament, and we would have one less intellectual stepping stone to the wisdom of the New.

For all his ruminations, Qoheleth never asks the question whether or not happiness *should* be the lot of man on earth. He resignedly assumes instead that life involves both unhappiness and happiness, and both have their turns on the rotating, fateful cycle that makes up human life. His pragmatic, world-weary attitude is that one should accommodate oneself to the hard fact that whether or not one seeks a life of virtue and wisdom, "blessings" from God are not to be expected here and now as a reward. This is evident to him from his personal experience — and this despite the common platitudes of more conservative wisdom literature (Proverbs and Sirach, for example). He encourages us, therefore, to find enjoyment in the routines of living ordinary life, enduring what cannot be altered.

So it is that he never poses an answer to the question of what we should *expect* from the hand of a just and merciful God. Are we *supposed* to be happy in this life? Are we *supposed* to be unhappy? Qoheleth merely counsels us to enjoy whatever lawful pleasures we are permitted in the providence of God. But the larger question still remains: What does God desire for us, especially for those who are believers and (like Job) maybe even *righteous?*

Ecclesiastes doesn't take on this grand question. The skeptical and melancholic book of Job, however, most emphatically does. Like Ecclesiastes, seen from a Christian perspective, it is also a *praeparatio evangelica,* and so we can expect it, similarly, to pose more questions than solutions. But, in some ways, Job is even more disturbing a work than Ecclesiastes, as we shall see. We turn to it next.

Chapter Five

Job and the Problem
of Conventional Piety

I N THE last chapter I had some things to say about "conventional piety." That begs the question, of course, of what "conventional piety" is, particularly where Ecclesiastes and now the book of Job are concerned.

"Conventional piety" here means a sort of religious moral reasoning common not only in ancient Hebrew faith, but also in earlier Mesopotamian religion. That it has persisted as an enduring belief is shown by its presence in many popular versions of Christianity even in our own day. Whenever you hear a radio preacher promise God's material blessings to those who give financially to his ministry, for example, there is an updated — and somewhat debased — popular version of it.

In short, it is the doctrine that practical righteousness invariably brings about God's benediction and prosperity in the life of the one doing good, and, contrariwise, un-righteousness brings about God's malediction and ruin for the perpetrator. Classic expressions of this doctrine, addressed to the Hebrew people as a whole, can be found in the Law of Moses — for example, in Leviticus 26 and Deuteronomy 28. Psalms 1 and 37 (36) are two examples of the same ethic as applied to individuals, and the books of Proverbs and Sirach simply assume this doctrine when they aren't asserting it explicitly.

The Bible, in other words, teaches "conventional piety." This alone should caution us against any temptation to discount it out of hand as being of little or no value. Surely, there is a non-negotiable and sensible measure of truth contained in it.

Plainly put, without the protective guidelines provided by a commonly held "conventional piety" or "conventional morality" of some sort, there would be very little stability either in a society such as ancient Israel's, or indeed in any civilized context. It undergirds distributive justice with the threat or promise of retributive justice, thus making the mutual practice of fair dealing and good behavior desirable, at least for the rewards these may bring. Not a particularly high rationale for morality, but an easily understood and digestible one.

All cultures have some form of "conventional piety" and "conventional wisdom" without which there could be no culture as such. In its absence, society would lack something essentially constituent and cohesive. It is a standard of justice, because morality must underpin law for the latter to be credible, and in this way it has an acknowledged place in maintaining good order. It is necessary to the fabric of any enduring society that nobody should be able simply to "get away with" downright evil or just plain shabby behavior. If one's neighbors don't see the perpetration of a misdemeanor, blow the whistle, and deal with the matter justly, then — so belief in the "conventional piety" of divine retribution would have it — God himself certainly will.

There is, however, a "dark side" to this way of thinking whenever it is taken too far. According to the teachings of conventional piety, the assumption is that the "good" are *supposed* to experience a measure of happiness, health, prosperity, and blessing; and the "wicked" are *supposed* to suffer loss, disease, misfortune, and God's curse. At its worst, when men take the exercising of responsibility for this in hand themselves, it can become the basis for oppressive legalism, harsh and fear-inducing penalties, loss of legitimate freedoms, a "police state," ruthless treatment of the guilty, mistaken condemning of the innocent, inquisitions, and so on — quite often "in the name of God."

Somewhat less intimidating, it can also lead to a sort

of mechanical thinking about how "God" operates, a dispassionate view of Divine Providence based on mere cause and effect. In other words, in conventionally pious thinking, it is assumed that we are *supposed* to be manifestly happy in this life, but that this *should only* be guaranteed if we are manifestly "righteous." So — how can we be *seen* to be righteous? Most clearly by the circumstances of our *observable* lives, wherein will be *seen* the rewards we have received from God, either in his blessing or in his curse.

This is, of course, very good news for those who are in fact wealthy, healthy, and honored, because their privileges in life appear to manifest publicly a condition of divine justification.

However, this is very bad news for those who are sick, blind, deaf, crippled, poor, or in any other evident condition of misfortune, whose outward state apparently displays their otherwise concealed personal sinfulness, or possibly some divine chastisement being visited upon a whole family line ("unto the third and fourth generation"). Those for whom Mother Teresa so devotedly gave herself would, on such grounds, be suffering from their own unrighteousness, or their lack of worshiping the true God, or some other "reason" related to God's severe judgment. And those countless thousands killed by tsunami, earthquake, flood, war, pestilence, disease, poverty, famine, and so on? On the basis of this sort of relentless and inexorable piety of reward and merit, all these would be the victims of their own moral or religious failures. There are those — Christians so-called — who have had the audacity to claim this very thing in the name of Jesus Christ!

But this is light years from the mind of Christ; and his alone is the standard of justice for the Christian.

Where this is concerned, there is a significant Gospel passage in which Jesus' disciples ask him about the man born blind: "Rabbi, who sinned, this man or his parents, that he was born blind?" (John 9:2). These same disciples, in another place, after Jesus teaches them that being rich not only may *not* be a blessing but may instead prove to be a barrier to entry into the Kingdom of God, respond with incredulity: "Who then can be saved?" (Matt. 19:25). As men brought up with the notion of conventional piety, they couldn't immediately grasp that, on the one occasion, a man's blindness did *not* mean that he or his parents had sinned and that his affliction was a punishment, or that, on a different occasion, another man's wealth was *not* an indication of blessing and salvation. This wasn't how things were *supposed* to be *in their eyes.* Blindness was *supposed* to be a punishment; wealth was *supposed* to be a godly reward. These were *supposed* to be obvious, visible things, manifesting God's pleasure or displeasure publicly. In fact, however, in all four Gospels Jesus shoots down any such consoling reliance on this sort of "mechanical thinking" or "visible justice" in the ways of God (see, for example, Luke 13:1-5; Matt. 5:45).

Thus, even though the Bible maintains the conservative wisdom of "conventional piety," both Testaments present a serious critique of it when it is taken too far. In other words, conventional piety is fine so far as it goes, but it doesn't go very far at all in making sense of the larger mystery enveloping our existence — it has significant limitations where "explaining" human experience is concerned. It cannot be a criterion of Truth, even if it is a minimal criterion for maintaining societal orderliness and morals. What relatively small truth it possesses can only intelligently be appreciated in relation to a much more expansive revelation of God.

That expansive and corrective revelation is necessary in view of this simple irrefutable datum: many righteous persons *do* suffer, and many unrighteous persons *do* get the goods in this world. It is obvious to anyone who looks out the window or pays attention to the daily news. It is a disappointing and dismal fact of life. Conventionally pious rhetoric aside, a simple walk through any town anywhere on earth proves the falsity of the claim that reward and punishment naturally or divinely concur here and now with any rules of justice. Sometimes it does seem as if things work out the *right* way, but at least just as often it appears otherwise. We are back to Qoheleth's more somber description of a "wheel of fate," a *perpetuum mobile.* But even that seems too "regular," too neat. This isn't the sort of world that can even depend on the predictability illustrated by the ancient and medieval concept of the Wheel of Fate, upon which what goes up *must* come down. Where misfortune, illness, disaster, and death are concerned, chaos is the paradoxical "order" of the day. Of one thing only can we be sure: the mortality rate remains steady at one hundred percent.

THE BOOK of Job takes up the very disturbing realization that conventional piety simply doesn't work as an absolute — this, despite the fact that the book in its final form, as we now have it, may have been structured on an older folk tale that was originally told to defend conventional piety. The date of the book has been debated and is inconclusive, though it is fairly undeniable that the final versions — I say "versions" because there are differences, most noticeably in length, between the Septuagint and Masoretic texts — are post-exilic. It is reputedly the most difficult of Old Testament books to translate, and any three translations looked at side-by-side will demonstrate just how great a variety of interpretations is possible for numerous verses.

As a character, Job was legendary or semi-legendary,

and he is mentioned twice elsewhere in the Bible, once in the Old Testament and once in the New. In Ezekiel 14:14 and 20, his name appears as someone who might normally be considered of particular influence as an intercessor with God, although the point of this particular prophetic text is that even he, along with Noah and Daniel, would be unable to sway the Lord to act mercifully in those circumstances demanding judgment to which Ezekiel refers.

In the New Testament, the Epistle of James commends Job for his steadfastness in adversity, emphasizing along with this particular virtue of his the "compassion" and "mercy" of the Lord (James 5:11).

The original folk story on which the book of Job is built, assuming there was such an original folk story at all, seems to have gone something like this: the Lord YHWH is holding court, and among his ministers is "the *satan*" ("the adversary" — in this sense, more a "devil's advocate" than the later traditional picture we have of "the Devil"). The *satan* proposes a trial of Job's renowned faith. Job, of course, cannot be aware of this heavenly wager, so throughout the story he desperately tries to understand his own subsequent predicament. Job 1:1 informs the reader that the protagonist is a "righteous gentile" from the land of Uz (probably the same as Edom), the nature of whose faith in God is therefore reminiscent of Abraham's.

God permits the *satan* two vicious assaults on his righteous servant, ultimately leaving Job in the condition of sitting on a dunghill, destitute of family and possessions, scraping at his boils with a pot-shard and being accosted by three accusatory friends. (Since the *satan* is Job's would-be accuser in heaven, it is worth noting that Job's three friends, along with his wife, do the work of the devil on the latter's behalf on earth.) Job nevertheless holds on to his trust in God throughout his ordeals. At the end of the story, he is rewarded by a double restitution to make up for all his lost former possessions, and his deceased seven sons and three daughters are replaced by seven new sons and three new daughters (the latter, we are told, being fair — 42:15). In addition, Job is given the priestly task of offering sacrifice, something we find him doing on behalf of his children in the first chapter, but now on behalf of his deservedly hangdog friends. The conclusion is that perseverance under trial results, if one endures to the very end, in just reward.

This, though, is but the merest skeleton upon which the flesh and sinews of the final version hang; and scholars are perhaps right to assume that, in the hands of some unknown poet or poets, the postulated popular folk tale was at some later date reworked into the startling disputation that now constitutes the bulk of the book. Indeed, after the second chapter the *satan* altogether disappears from the story, his role behind the scenes all but forgotten. The central issue is now entirely that of the relationship of God and man.

AND HERE there is not the religious ethical optimism one finds in such biblical texts as the book of Proverbs or the first and thirty-seventh Psalms. Even when this kind of optimism is espoused by the three friends of Job, their optimism is shown to be intellectually shallow, a thin varnish on the surface of vastly more profound mysteries. Although what is presumed to be the original ending of the story of Job remains intact — Job perseveres in his faith and is restored twofold by God for doing so — what one ultimately takes away from this remarkable book is the disturbing revelation that the righteous can and do suffer and the unrighteous can and do prosper in this world, and that God's ways in these matters are not "mechanical" but free and unfathomable by the mind of man.

It is therefore a thoroughly *skeptical* book, in that it looks long, hard, and critically at things as they really are — in this case the terrible, divinely sanctioned ordeal of faith that Job undergoes; and it explores in the face of that hard reality every possible avenue of explanation.

The conventional piety of Job's three friends, Eliphaz the Temanite, Bildad the Shuhite, and Zophar the Naamathite, is pushed to the very limit of its capacity to explain what has happened to the book's righteous protagonist. Job can do little more than bewail his condition and call God to account for it, and near the end of his lamentations he comes quite dangerously close to condemning God's ways. Job the patient becomes increasingly Job the impatient. Only the young, inexplicably present interloper, Elihu the Buzite, elevates the entire argument to the different, more expansive perspective so urgently required.

As the three friends' speeches progressively degenerate into ever more and more hysterical and groundless accusation, asserting that the suffering of Job must certainly prove his wickedness, there being no other possible explanation for it within their conventional religious theory (e.g., Eliphaz's unrestrained charges against Job's character in Chapter 22), Job can only bewail the dark sense he has of God's absence (e.g., Chapter 23) and his anguish in wanting a direct explanation from God. Job persists in being both a *skeptic* — skeptical of the pat religious answers and religiously grounded accusations of his "comforters," who seek (absurdly) to defend God himself — and clearly a *man of faith* who refuses to allow the matter of his innocent suffering to go without explanation from a just God. Indeed, he pushes his case to the limit and brings down in a whirlwind the thunderous response he thinks he yearns to hear.

Likewise, the book of Job is a *melancholy* book. Job's words addressed to God are in the form of a lament, filled with mourning and longing. It is enlightening to note that at times Job speaks to God directly, while his friends theorize about God but never address him. They are the theologians, the scholastics, the pedants, those who think themselves capable of justifying the ways of God to man. They are, though, wrong in all their theories and formulae. Meanwhile, in the face of their ever more desperate and heavy-handed efforts, and even while Job experiences what seems to be the absence of God, Job's faith presses him on, paradoxically, to call on God anyway. There is an embedded irony throughout the debate well worth noting here: *It is the **melancholy** of Job over the perceived injustice of his circumstances that pushes him to call out to God in **faith**; while it is the black-and-white **moral certainty** of his friends, seen in their conventionally pious theories about God and the presumed causes of Job's afflictions, which moves them to **condemn** their friend.*

JOB'S FRIENDS, in fact, act from *pride*.

Obviously, we are quite close to the spirit of the Gospel with this particular insight. One is put in mind of the warnings of Jesus that we ought not to judge others, that we are to remove the blinding log from our own eyes before attempting to remove the speck from another's, that we are always unprofitable servants and mustn't parade our righteousness in public, and so on. The parable in Luke 18:9-14, about the self-righteous Pharisee and the repenting and lamenting tax collector in the temple, illustrates a similar point about judging others while assuming one's own good standing before God (although, unlike Job, the repentant tax collector had a guilty conscience). Likewise, there is the grumpy older brother of Luke 15:11-32, who cannot bear to see his younger brother's full — and, in his eyes, inappropriate — reinstatement by his indulgent father. (Again, unlike Job, the younger son actually had some grave matters to regret.) *Mixed with uncritical moral certainty, one based solely on religious theory and conventionally pious assumptions, is often the leaven of pride.*

To be sure, there is "good" pride and "bad" pride. Defining *pride* in the latter sense is difficult. It should not, for instance, be confused with "self-centeredness." Everyone is "self-centered," since each of us has no other "self" to be centered in other than the self we are. At our most outwardly directed, most loving and generous, even at our most God-focused, we are operating out of our unique selves as from a "central location." Similarly, pride in our abilities and achievements, to the extent that these are recognized to be gifts we have utilized well, is not "bad" pride. The Pharisee in the temple, for example, wasn't wrong in having done his good works before God. If he had considered himself "an unprofitable servant" and hadn't stuck his nose in the tax collector's business, he would have been just fine. No, he went away without being justified because he thought he *merited a reward* from God for doing his good works (that is to say, he thought he was doing Almighty God a much-appreciated favor), and — far worse still — because he judged the tax collector in the process of praising himself.

There is a form of pride that is essentially evil precisely because it is draped in conventional religion, and thus goes undetected because it looks so harmless and respectable. This sort of pride, what we see in the Pharisee in the temple and also among Job's friends, *is the objectifying of others — not really seeing others as persons in their own right, but as objects whose value we feel we have the right to evaluate.*

One is reminded that St. Paul didn't even believe he had the right to evaluate himself, despite the obvious fact that he knew himself better than any other human being did — God alone being the Judge of every individual person (1 Cor. 4:3-4; cf. James 4:11-12). Paul knew he was far too complicated a soul for his own self-appraisal to be either an accurate one or able to provide enough evidence for a sound verdict. There is always danger in presuming to climb into God's throne to judge another or oneself, not the least danger being the inability of one to know a human soul inside and out, which means that one must inevitably judge on the basis of a knowledge he cannot possibly ever possess. This is pride of the worst sort. *Actions* can and must be judged on occasion — they can be objectified; but *persons* should not be judged — they cannot be objectified. That is the sole prerogative of God, who sees the human person in all his complexity.

The tendency to *objectify persons* made in the image of God is also the evil at the heart of *sexual lust* (not to be confused with healthy sexual desire), which is the opposite of love because it reduces people to the level of commodities — objects existing for our own gratification. Whenever we perceive other human beings as ciphers, things, aliens, consumers, consumables, or pigeonhole them in simple categories, one can be sure that something deeply evil is at work in us, whether it manifests itself as lust or pride.

Pride is one type of that condition the Bible calls "hardness of heart." Under the disguise provided by conventional piety, it is not at all as obvious or troubling a thing to the religious individual as sexual lust, for instance, might be. A religious person may rightly be appalled and made anxious upon discovering the disruptive movements of lust within himself or herself; but that

87

same person might not even notice the interior presence of a truly malignant pride.

Pride of the worst sort views others as an audience, or perhaps as a mere crowd of faceless nonentities best avoided or openly despised. It is the inability of one "self" to recognize others as "other selves." Others are depersonalized, categorized, dismissed, accepted, and so on, all on the basis of one's own presuppositions. It doesn't really *see* another; it *filters* another through an invisible mental mesh. This is the subtle sin of Job's three friends. *What they see and what they think they see are two entirely different things.* On the basis of conventional piety, they think they see God's wrath being exercised, but Job knows otherwise. *What they see is an illusion, one born from theory alone.*

These would-be "comforters" actually fail, therefore, to see Job at all; what they see, rather, is Job's *situation.* Since his *situation* matches only their conventional presuppositions regarding the effects of divine judgment on evil, they assert — and go on asserting with ever-increasing belligerency, despite Job's protestations and prayers — that their categorization of Job as "a sinner cursed by God" is the only possible explanation of what they observe. Job is rendered thereby an "object" — indeed, an "object lesson" — one whose problems can be interpreted as a "Sunday school" illustration of how "being bad" leads to misery, and "being good" leads to happiness. However, this superficial "Sunday school lesson" will be overturned in the book, first by the youthful and blustery Elihu, and ultimately by God himself, who shows up in a cyclone to answer Job directly. Job's prayer has been all along that God, *who does see him* and not just his situation, will come personally and vindicate him — and God does.

WHAT IS also notably sad in the case of Job's *friends* is their failure to honor the nature of *friendship,* something Job could reasonably have expected from them. Instead, their pride and piety and "orthodox" theories undermine their ability to show him any true sympathy. What is certainly their genuinely felt initial distress at seeing Job in his predicament degenerates into theological lectures, reproaches, and wrangling. Job's real disappointment in view of their failure to befriend him at his moment of greatest need is bitterly stated in more than one place. "My brethren are treacherous as a torrent-bed. . . . In time of heat they disappear," he laments. "Such you have now become to me; you see my calamity, and are afraid" (6:15, 17, 21). In language reminiscent of Psalm 88 (87), he says, "[God] has put my brethren far from me, and my acquaintances are wholly estranged from me. My kinsfolk and my close friends have failed me. . . . All my intimate friends abhor me, and those whom I loved have turned against me" (19:13-14, 19). And he cries out to his companions in utter discouragement, "Have pity on me, have pity on me, O you my friends, for the hand of God has touched me!" (19:21).

Job has a singular *need* for his friends during this time of crisis. It's not a "need" for explanations or recriminations, for bombastic theorizing or for the issuing of repetitious calls for him to "repent." He has no need for them to tell him about the ways of God, which he knows better than they, or for them to advise him on how to get right with the Almighty. He has merely the need for them to be *with* him and to give him support during the trial of his faith. He has the need to be treated as a *person* — troubled, yes, but still trusting God. He could benefit from the quiet presence of their own faith exercised in humility. We might say that he requires their love, if we mean by "love" something stripped of sentimentality — that is, something which is practical and of service to the one in pain. But that need is not met by these supposed "friends," increasing thereby the weight of Job's sorrows. Instead of helping him to bear up under his burden, they increase the load that's already crushing him. Even more than Qoheleth, Job expresses the deep human need for friendship by decrying its betrayal.

Job and the Problem of Conventional Piety

ONE CAN get the picture if one recognizes the sheer darkness of mind Job is undergoing in the story. God is suddenly silent and absent after a series of what to Job are inexplicable disasters. His wife has told him to curse God and die. His children are dead. His friends have become his accusers. He is isolated, alienated from everyone, including — it seems — God, in whom he trusted; and when his friends are finally rendered dumb by Job's persistence in claiming innocence, all he then sees before him are their blank expressions, but he experiences no comfort. Job sits stuck on a road going nowhere in the blackness of isolation. He is impoverished and infinitely lonely. He can't move forward or turn back the clock. No one is there who has either the will or the power to help him; and he feels himself to be dying. It is a frightful mess, a horrible state of mind.

A Christian is, of course, immediately put in mind of Jesus in Gethsemane, his forsakenness after the flight of his friends, the subsequent three denials of Peter in the courtyard, and the supreme dereliction of the crucified Christ: "My God, my God, why have you abandoned me?" The darkness of Job is a foreshadowing of the darkness of the cross.

However, there is a most important difference: in the case of Jesus, we find *God* himself on the cross and forsaken. In Job's case, however, he is overwhelmed by God when the

Almighty appears to him in the blast of the whirlwind: "Behold, I am vile; what shall I answer thee? I will lay mine hand upon my mouth. Once have I spoken; but I will not answer: yea, twice; but I will proceed no further. . . . I uttered [what] I understood not; things too wonderful for me, which I knew not. . . . I have heard of thee by the hearing of the ear: but now mine eye seeth thee. Wherefore I abhor myself, and repent in dust and ashes" (40:4-5; 42:3, 5-6, KJV).

Despite the differences between Jesus and Job, it is nonetheless the same God, taking up the magnificent old skeptical/melancholic poetic fable of Job and making it a portion of his "Word" to us, who in the context of the story confounds Job by his majesty and mystery and mythological baby-talk, who later makes himself present definitively and solemnly in "the Word made flesh." Of him, reminiscent of the sufferings of Job, we read such things as this: "And the scripture was fulfilled, which saith, And he was numbered with the transgressors. And they that passed by railed on him, wagging their heads. . . . Likewise also the chief priests mocking said among themselves with the scribes, He saved others; himself he cannot save . . ." (Mark 15:28-31, KJV). The Lord of the whirlwind, whose pets are Behemoth and Leviathan, is finally seen in time in a condition more bitter than that of the legendary Job. Not only, then, is the darkness of Job a foreshadowing of the cross, but even more to the point, the cross is ultimately God's

truest answer to the cries of Job and to the book as a whole
— much more so than the "happy ending" of Job 42. The divine speech from the cyclone takes place simply to dis-
perse man's meager theories about the ways of God, not to
"explain" those ways, "because the foolishness of God is
wiser than men, and the weakness of God is stronger than
men" (1 Cor. 1:25, KJV). The book of Job, like that of Ecclesiastes, is an incomplete revelation, pointing to the fuller
revelation of God in Christ. "The world by wisdom knew
not God.... But we preach Christ crucified ... the power of
God, and the wisdom of God" (1 Cor. 1:21-24, KJV).

Christ is ultimately the *Friend* that Job's three friends
are not. He reveals God's solidarity with human suffering.
The *pride* that *objectifies* others in the name of religion —
the potential danger in any conventional piety — is ban-
ished in the *humility* of God that *identifies* with our sorrows, weaknesses, degradation, and death. "Greater love
has no man than this, that a man lay down his life for his
friends" (John 15:13). To "bear one another's burdens" is
"the *law* of Christ" (Gal. 6:2, italics mine), a very different
sort of law than that proposed by a rigidly conventional
legal theory of "reward and punishment."

Christ is the Friend who, in a sense, takes Job's place
on the wretched dunghill on his behalf: "Christ redeemed
us from the curse of the law, having become a curse for
us" (Gal. 3:13). He is the Lord who descends to us to lift us

up together with himself. "Who is like unto the Lord our God, that hath his dwelling so high: and yet humbleth himself to behold the things that are in heaven and earth? He taketh up the simple out of the dust: and lifteth the poor out of the mire" (Ps. 113 [112]:5-6, Coverdale Psalter).

If the love of friendship is defined as the giving of one's self for the sake of others, as Jesus teaches, then such "friends" as the "friends" of Job have much to learn, and Jesus is the perfect model of genuine friendship. Such demonstrated *love* as this engenders a person's committed *faith* (*pistis* = "trust"). In the words of the Apostle Paul, "The life I now live in the flesh I live by faith in the Son of God, *who loved me and gave himself for me*" (Gal. 2:20, italics mine). If we are looking for an objective, visible, and true manifestation of God's authentic brand of justice at work, a place for trust and real piety to begin in us, it is with the cross of Christ.

WHERE THE ending of the book of Job leaves us largely unsatisfied, the Gospel of Christ picks up. In Christ the melancholy of Job is supremely met by divine friendship, and his skepticism is accordingly able to move beyond anguished questioning in the direction of faith. Friendship and faith are the terms — personal terms — that transcend the meager categories of conventional piety.

They are terms that have to do with covenant and commitment and the laying down of one's life for another.

In what follows, we will in turn look at *friendship* in the life of faith, as — in Christ and under the cross — it is a gift given to strengthen us in our sorrows and questionings of God.

Chapter Six

A Midwinter's Dark Night Dialogue on Friendship

For a Christian, there are, strictly speaking, no chances. A secret Master of the Ceremonies has been at work. Christ, who said to the disciples, "Ye have not chosen me, but I have chosen you," can truly say to every group of Christian friends, "You have not chosen one another but I have chosen you for one another."... At this feast it is He who has spread the board, and it is He who has chosen the guests.

C. S. Lewis,
The Four Loves

A different version of this chapter originally appeared in *Touchstone* in 2002.

A Midwinter's Dark Night Dialogue on Friendship

*I recall now two friends, who, although they have
passed from this present life, nevertheless live to me
and always will so live.*

St. Aelred of Rievaulx,
Spiritual Friendship, 3:119

"ARISTOTLE ASKED an interesting question regarding the limits of friendship." This was spoken quietly over the empty plates. Dirk, a dog resembling a small
black-and-white bear in the light, could not now be seen,
except as a darker blur against the room's shadows. He
could be heard, however, in a corner, licking clean the
meat platter that had considerately been placed on the
floor for him. The only light came from two candles on
the dining room table and a fire in the nearby hearth.

About the table sat four men and two women. I was
there, and my two oldest friends, my comrades since
school days, John and Jerome. Jerome was a fine artist, especially in oils and sculpture, but now working in com-
puter graphics design. John was a chef, gifted in the prep-
aration and presentation of food and wine, and working
at a renowned restaurant in Baltimore. I had known both
of these men since we were teenagers together.

There, too, was my relatively recent friend from Nor-
way, an iconographer and art historian named Solrunn.

It seemed a bit unusual for me to see her there among our company. I remember this passing awareness, which lasted but a moment, because until that evening I had had no reason to suspect she was at all acquainted with the others present. In fact, I would previously have said that she was not. But, no, evidently she was; for here she sat, wearing a gray-black rabbit-fur vest and conversing happily with us all on familiar terms.

The other woman present was a nun in her seventies, dressed in traditional Benedictine-style black habit and veil. This was Mother Catherine Grace, a long-standing friend and spiritual counselor of nearly thirty years, soon to retire from her position as superior of her monastic community. Her presence exuded a sense of serenity in the room, an aspect of her character that effortlessly flowed from her disciplined and contemplative spirit.

The fourth man, the eldest among us and the most striking in appearance, was wearing a black cassock, his hair and beard gray-white. This was Father Haire, and the rest of us were visiting him in the Hermitage.

Outdoors, night had fallen, a chill wind was blowing through the leafless woods nearby, and a wet snow was coming down. Indoors, all was relaxed and comfortable. The meal was concluded, but we still sat with glasses of wine and a half-full bottle, and still another uncorked besides.

A Midwinter's Dark Night Dialogue on Friendship

Father Haire was the chaplain for the convent on the hilltop. To visit the grounds of this convent from time to time, where the chaplain's Hermitage was located, was to experience the intimation that we had stepped into another world. To be here was to leave the world "out there," to be *some place else,* a place that had the atmosphere of the ancient and ageless.

Jerome, John, and I had become well-acquainted with Father Haire many years before, and we enjoyed our occasional meals and conversations with him. He enjoyed playing the host, and we benefited by moving him to share his spiritual insights. Solrunn's presence was an added pleasure, since one could always depend on her to ask provocative questions and to make unexpected, keen-edged observations. Mother Catherine Grace would bring the wisdom acquired from prayer and the experience of guiding others in community — and also the personal experience born of suffering from cancer. We were, therefore, a gathering made up of various ages, both sexes, different ways of living, none of us connected to each other by blood or marriage, or even — in one case — nationality; in other words, a true *fellowship* of Christian friends in miniature.

And in fact we had gotten onto the topic of Christian friendship. I mentioned that I had been thinking and writing about Ecclesiastes and the book of Job, and that friendship had come up as a subject, particularly in the case of Job. I repeated some of my thoughts on the subject, noting how it seemed crucial to Job to have his friends' encouragement and yet how sadly his friends had failed him in the context of his crises. Christian (or "spiritual") friendship was a subject that interested us, our own amity having begun with Christ firmly at the center of our respective lives, despite our differences of official affiliation. Two of us were Roman Catholics (Solrunn and I), two were Eastern Orthodox (John and Jerome), and Father Haire and Mother Catherine Grace, along with her sisters over at the convent on the hill, were Anglicans. All of us maintained our ecclesiastical convictions, yet our Christ-centered friendship was no less strong for that.

So the conversation had begun in earnest with Father Haire, warming to the subject, while the winter wind whistled outside and the snow fell.

"Aristotle asked an interesting question regarding the limits of friendship," Father Haire said. "He said that there are natural limits to friendship whenever a great inequality between friends is realized. He asked whether or not we could wish for our friends 'the greatest of all goods, namely, *to be gods*.' It's a fascinating question. Would we really ever want our friends, our companions and 'equals' to be *gods?* Friendship, Aristotle assumed, can *only* exist between equals, so he answered his question in the negative. He said that 'when one partner is quite separated from the other, as in the case of divinity, the friendship can remain no longer.'"[1]

Father Haire poured a bit more wine into our glasses and continued. "But Aristotle saw things, understandably, from a pagan and pre-Christian point of view. He couldn't possibly have conceived the later Christian idea of God the Son — deity in the ultimate sense — bridging the chasm of absolute inequality between man and God in himself.

"Of course, it isn't the case that we mortal creatures could ever really become 'divine' (whatever that might mean) — and certainly not on our own steam. Aristotle thus posed a question that no one needs to get very exercised about. No one would be capable of such a thing. But God, on the other hand, or so Christians believe, *did become man.* The revelation of Christ makes that bold assertion; and that's precisely, I think, where friendship between Christians finds its bedrock — as does everything else in Christian life. *Friendship in Christ,* as the New Testament suggests, particularly in the Gospel of John, is based on something specified as *friendship with Christ* — and that in turn could only be as *unequal* a friendship as one might possibly imagine. In the ancient world, friendship could

1. Aristotle, *Nicomachean Ethics,* 1159a, 1ff.

only exist among equals; the Christian message is — in contradistinction to that — saying something else."

Father Haire took a sip of his wine. "From the outset, Christianity said that Christ's friendship raises human nature up, in a way Aristotle could not have guessed, 'to become by grace what he himself is by nature.' In other words, he condescended to us to lift us up to heaven, to make us (if you will) *gods by grace.* In other words, by friendship with one who is vastly, infinitely *superior* to us, we are lifted to a sort of '*equal* status' through his grace. Christianity consequently redefines 'friendship.' 'Equality' per se ceases to be based on social strata, race, intelligence, gender, personal achievement, material acquisition, shared tastes, or anything else we possess by virtue of our natural birth. Rather, equality is assumed to exist between all human beings — Jew and Gentile, slave and free, male and female — because all are 'one in Christ,' in whom the various chasms of inequality are forever bridged (see Gal. 3:28; Col. 3:11; Rom. 10:12). It's an *equality of shared destiny,* to become *together* like Christ; and so our equality is based on grace and in relation to God in Christ. Whatever our backgrounds, differences, personal deficiencies, conditions of birth, and so on, we are nonetheless equal in our *calling,* and thus friendship can be extended to all. It's an understanding of both equality and friendship that Aristotle wouldn't recognize."

Jerome leaned back in his chair, and then said, "I recall that C. S. Lewis noted in his famous book, *The Four Loves,* how infrequently friendship, or *philia,* is used in Scripture as an image of the love between God and man. He wrote that familial 'affection is taken as the image when God is represented as our Father; *eros* when Christ is represented as the Bridegroom of the Church.' I think he even says that Scripture very nearly 'ignores' friendship as an analogy, though it doesn't neglect it altogether."[2]

Father Haire reached down to Dirk, who was now lying by his foot, scratched behind one of the dog's ears, and replied, "Well, C. S. Lewis was surely right when he referred to *agape* as Love itself — in the New Testament the word is used for God's love, all-embracing, self-giving, self-sacrificing, and the source of all loves. Familial affection and *eros* give us needed insights into God's love. But so, too, does friendship, and perhaps it pre-eminently does so. I tend to think that C. S. Lewis, despite the fact that his chapter on friendship contains many valuable insights, nonetheless shortchanges the concept a bit. I don't think that because something is mentioned only a few times in Scripture it is therefore 'ignored' or unim-

2. C. S. Lewis, *The Four Loves* (New York: Harcourt Brace Jovanovich, 1960), p. 78.

portant. Besides, Jesus certainly reflects the rather common classical view that friendship *(philia)* is the greatest expression of *agape* (John 15:13). Christ is the true Friend of the Christian soul. He says, after all, 'You are my friends' and 'I have called you friends' in John 15:14-15. He makes himself the standard and archetype for every other friendship."

After a short moment of silence, Mother Catherine Grace spoke gently. "It is St. Aelred of Rievaulx," she said, "the twelfth-century English abbot, who might for us be called the 'Doctor of Friendship.' He was someone who deeply understood the value of friendship in Christ, how to define it, and what its relationship is to God's love. His monastery of Rievaulx was a place where friendship was not only allowed to develop among the members of the community, but was positively encouraged. It's a shame that some later monastic practice, fearful of 'particular friendships' giving way to sexual misbehavior (which, of course, can be a problem), tended to throw the baby out with the bath water, forbidding healthy friendships along with potentially unhealthy ones. Anyway, if you can, take time to read Aelred's two books, *The Mirror of Charity* and *Spiritual Friendship.* You won't regret working through them, or anything else written by him, for that matter."

"How would Aelred relate friendship to *agape,* then?" asked Jerome.

"Since, for the Christian," responded Mother Catherine Grace, "all love is based on the love of God (*agape* or *caritas,* 'charity'), Aelred — as I understand him — says that friendship (*philia* or *amicitia*) is rooted in, and revelatory of, that." She produced, as if by magic, a copy of Aelred's *Spiritual Friendship.*

"For example, Aelred says here that 'what is true of charity, I surely do not hesitate to grant to friendship, since "he that abides in friendship, abides in God, and God in him,"' and 'God is friendship.'[3] These are quite strong words, implying that, at heart, *agape* and *philia* cannot be dissociated in the mind of the Christian. For Aelred, the latter is — or should be — the pure expression of the former.

"So it is that Aelred dismisses what he calls 'worldly' and 'carnal' friendships, even going so far as denying them the quality of true friendship. He can do this because he sees 'friendship' as fully defined by the revelation of Jesus himself. And why not? It's what Father Haire was saying a moment ago. In light of the Incarnation, everything becomes subject to redefinition. Redefined, then, *friendship* for the follower of Jesus must accordingly be something leading to, or assisting, a person's salva-

3. St. Aelred of Rievaulx, *Spiritual Friendship,* trans. M. E. Laker (Kalamazoo: Cistercian Publications, 1974), 1:70, 69; 3:5, 54; cf. 1 John 4:16.

tion. Aelred says that it *begins* in Christ, *continues* in Christ, and finds its *perfection* in Christ.[4] Elsewhere, still filling out the definition, as it were, he writes, after being asked what should be the limits of true — that is, 'spiritual' or Christian — friendship, 'Christ himself set up a definite goal for friendship when he said: "Greater love than this no man hath, that a man lay down his life for his friends." See how far love between friends should extend; namely, that they be willing to die for one another. Does that seem adequate to you?'[5]

"For Aelred, each flesh-and-blood friend is a gift given by Christ of particular individuals to particular individuals. In other words, no healthy 'spiritual' friendship is ever a sheer coincidence, but rather the work of providence — one through which Christ shows us his own friendship. Christ, says Aelred, inspires the love of friends for one another, and therefore it is holy and should be maintained in holiness."

Mother Catherine Grace set the book down on the table and leaned back, her face in shadow now, though her eyes shone with the light from the candles. "Ideally, friendship becomes a means to Christ, a 'ladder' to heaven. Aelred writes, near the end of his book, 'Was it

4. St. Aelred of Rievaulx, *Spiritual Friendship,* 1:9.
5. St. Aelred of Rievaulx, *Spiritual Friendship,* 2:33.

not a foretaste of blessedness thus to love and thus to be loved; thus to help and thus to be helped; and in this way from the sweetness of fraternal charity to wing one's flight aloft to that more sublime splendor of divine love, and by the ladder of charity now to mount to the embrace of Christ himself; and again to descend to the love of neighbor, there pleasantly to rest?'"[6]

I was curious how it was she could quote so extensively from such a text without bothering to look up passages.

Seeing that Mother Catherine Grace had finished her thought, Father Haire then picked up the theme: "*Agape* could easily appear to us to be only a general sort of love: 'For God so *loved* the *world*'; 'he maketh his sun to rise on the evil *and* on the good'; 'God commendeth his *love* toward us, in that, *while we were yet sinners,* Christ died for us'; and so on (John 3:16; Matt. 5:45; Rom. 5:8, KJV). Such verses as these tell us of the *universal, nonparticular* character of *agape.* We should also take note of the fact that when followers of Christ are taught, for example, to 'love their enemies' (Matt. 5:44), it is an exhortation to mirror God's long-suffering, universal *agape* — certainly not a call to become intimate acquaintances with them.

"But *philia* — friendship — takes us from this general

6. St. Aelred of Rievaulx, *Spiritual Friendship,* 3:127.

love of *agape* to the specifically personal: each soul in his or her uniqueness and particularity is potentially the friend of Christ. This is the call to discipleship, to which each person, like Peter and Andrew and James and John, on his own must respond. *Philia* lies behind the most demanding words of Jesus in the Gospels, addressed to individuals: 'He that loveth father or mother more than me is not worthy of me; and he that loveth son or daughter more than me is not worthy of me. And he that taketh not his cross, and followeth after me, is not worthy of me. He that findeth his life shall lose it; and he that loseth his life for my sake shall find it' (Matt. 10:37-39, KJV). This is even more directly put in John's Gospel: 'Greater love *(agapen)* hath no man than this, that a man lay down his life for his *friends (philon)*' (John 15:13)."

John, a mountain of a man, who had been sitting quietly up to this point, was holding his wineglass in his hand in a way that looked ludicrously delicate. "This wine has good legs," he muttered, peering through the glass at the candlelight. One expected such offhand comments now and then from a chef and wine connoisseur, and we would have resumed the conversation where Father Haire had left it, but John uncharacteristically continued to speak.

"This reminds me of an interesting image," he said. He extracted, as if from nowhere, a copy of the Faber and

Faber volume titled *Early Fathers from the Philokalia.*
(Just where these books came from, which Mother
Catherine Grace and now John so effortlessly produced,
did not concern me at the time. Later it would become
evident to me why it seemed so perfectly normal that
they could do so.)

"This comes from St. Dorotheos of Gaza, an abbot of
the sixth and seventh centuries," said John, finding his
place. He began to read:

> Imagine a circle with its centre and radii or rays go-
> ing out from this centre. The further these radii are
> from the centre, the more widely are they dispersed
> and separated from one another; and conversely,
> the closer they come to the centre, the closer they
> are to one another. Suppose now that this circle is
> the world, the very centre of the circle, God, and the
> lines (radii) going from the centre to the circumfer-
> ence or from the circumference to the centre are
> the paths of men's lives. Then here we see the same.
> Insofar as the saints move inwards within the circle
> towards its centre, wishing to come near to God,
> then, in the degree of their penetration, they come
> closer both to God and to one another; moreover,
> inasmuch as they come nearer to God, they come
> nearer to one another, and inasmuch as they come

nearer to one another, they come nearer to God. It is the same with drawing away. When they draw away from God and turn toward external things, it is clear that in the degree that they recede from the central point and draw away from God, they withdraw from one another, and as they withdraw from one another, so they draw away from God. Such is also the property of love; inasmuch as we are outside and do not love God, so each is far from his neighbor. But if we love God, inasmuch as we come near to Him by love of Him, so we become united by love with our neighbors, and inasmuch as we are united with our neighbours, so we become united with God.[7]

John closed the book and said, "This is a good illustration of *agape,* I think. The circle may be, as St. Dorotheos says, the world; but he might also have said it was the whole body of the redeemed throughout the world (and heaven, too). It's a vision of *koinonia* as seen with the eyes of faith. Love of God and neighbor are held together by a common focus on God himself — or, we would no doubt prefer to emphasize, on God Incarnate, Jesus Christ.

7. *Early Fathers from the Philokalia,* trans. E. Kadloubovsky and G. E. H. Palmer (London: Faber & Faber, Ltd., 1954), pp. 164-65.

"Each Sunday, after the Divine Liturgy, when everyone else has gone downstairs for coffee, I like to remain sitting in the church before the icons for awhile, looking especially upon the face of Christ; after all, 'the light of the knowledge of the glory of God [is] in the face of Jesus Christ' (2 Cor. 4:6). And that's where *philia* is best realized for me, and I mean specifically *friendship with Christ.*

"What Christ shares with us — what makes this a *friendship* involving real mutuality — is his own transfiguring glory, which conforms us to his image (Rom. 8:29; 2 Cor. 3:18). In other words, he gives his friends a share in his Spirit. But St. Dorotheos also describes each man's individual life, with his own individual commitment and individual loyalty, as a line drawn from the circumference to the center. Our personal lives are moving along those distinct lines either toward Christ or away from him. For us to move thus nearer to him, we must each have an individual, unique, developing friendship with him, which cannot be shared with any other human being (as some of the saints said of this relationship, 'My secret is my own'), and yet it is this reality that we have in common with all other disciples of Christ. . . ."

Jerome and I looked at each other with eyebrows arched. We weren't used to hearing John expound firsthand on deep things, which he usually kept close to his chest. On those extremely rare occasions when he did so speak, we found ourselves speechless, as indeed we did now.

"Anyway," John went on, "closeness to Christ draws us closer to each other in Christ. Universally, this is true, of course, of the whole, vast Christian *koinonia* in heaven and on earth. But if we believe that the Lord also provides particular Christian friendships for each of us in particular times and places — bringing together those who mutually sustain and fortify their spiritual lives through God-given ties, making them more than simply comrades — then we might also rightly see in this a sacramental microcosm of the universal *koinonia*. Friendship in Christ, made tangible within the smaller circle of good and lifelong friends, is providential. True Christian friends come to us as gifts from our greatest Friend, at the same time making us spiritual gifts to them. And what defines such a circle of friends — what is mutual between them — is, of course, friendship with Christ.

"So, whereas some might place it nearer the periphery of spiritual life, I believe friendship is the best picture of divine love among disciples. It is also profoundly biblical. Friendship was, after all, important for Christ during his earthly ministry. Think of John, the Beloved Disciple, and James, and Peter, and Lazarus and his sisters. If it was important for him, it can't be unimportant for us."

"But I can't help remembering those disappointing

friends of Job," I countered, looking out at the darkness beyond the icy windowpanes. "If not exactly 'friends in Christ,' they might still be considered something quite similar — his 'godly friends,' perhaps. And yet they failed him, holding before his eyes, as they did, a number of pious assumptions that — instead of lifting him up — tended to bury him deeper in his misery. They meant well, it seems, but it was precisely the very nature of their 'spirituality' or 'religion' that sank him. And I think some of us have had — or even possibly have been, in retrospect — 'friends of Job' at some time."

"I can think of one time," Jerome said quietly, "when we were like Job's friends toward John."

"And, because we have known each other since we were young and zealous," I replied, "I remember acting that way toward you. More than once."

"But, even so, here we are." Jerome slapped me on the shoulder. "It shows that even such misguided behavior doesn't necessarily end friendship. But isn't it interesting that what eventually needs forgiveness in such cases isn't whatever the person who is at the receiving end of such 'piety' may have done or not done, but rather the harsh or proud 'piety' itself? In the end, Job's friends are rebuked by God for speaking senselessly, and Job himself must offer sacrifices on their behalf."

Solrunn, my Norwegian iconographer friend, had all

this time been sitting with legs crossed and hands folded on her lap, looking from one speaker to the next. She now leaned forward, drank a little from her glass, and said, "In the end, speaking isn't the most important mark of friendship. Being with and standing by someone is. That's what gains trust and confidence in someone else, allowing the other person to be the unique person he or she is in a relaxed manner. One can do this even over a distance, as we know. 'Being with' someone is a matter of mind, intention, and communication. But communication between friends is something that expresses full acceptance of the other person, highs and lows, strengths and weaknesses, at many levels.

"There is a fjord in the Hardanger region where I come from called Simadalsfjord, just by Eidfjord. About six hundred meters above Simadalsfjord, located on a very steep mountain, is a rolling meadow and a farm called Kjeåsen (which means 'Goat Hill'). It's been there since the fourteenth century, settled by people from Bergen who were escaping the Black Death. It's an attraction now for tourists because it affords a remarkable view of the surrounding area — in my opinion, the most beautiful in the world; but I'm rather biased.

"One can, of course, drive up there and visit the farm. But there is another way up, a very steep and very challenging path. To get up that path, one needs to climb over rocks, ascend ladders, walk along narrow wooden planks on sheer rock, and use ropes to pull oneself up at the steepest places. It is demanding and tiring, but rewarding if one has the stamina for it." Solrunn smiled broadly at the memory of something, then went on.

"I think the ascent to Kjeåsen might be a picture of life and faith. Like Kjeåsen, life is rewarding in many ways — the view is good and worth the climb. But, without company, the ascent might prove so demanding as to become discouraging. When the muscles start aching, the sweat starts pouring, and one looks up at how much further there is to go instead of looking down at how far one has already come, then one might begin to question what the point is. What seemed at first to be a joy, worthwhile, a challenge to be embraced, instead begins to seem meaningless and purposeless. Faith in the vision to come, when one finally collapses in the meadow at the top and surveys inner Hardanger's magnificence, seems so far away and impractical that one can begin to question if the endeavor is worth the effort. Maybe it won't be so wonderful after all. Maybe it's someone's imagination that made it sound so exciting at first. Why not just turn around and go back down and simply drive up there instead?

"But, if one does that, one misses a lot. There's joy in a climb, after all, things to see around each and every bend;

and even if the muscles hurt and the sweat pours, it's worth it. But loneliness means the joy and the pain are not shared. You see it by yourself, and maybe you would wish to see it in company with someone else. That's when climbing to Kjeåsen with a friend might be sufficient encouragement to keep one going right on up to the very top, right to the summit and the green meadow and a staggering view of the world.

"I think life is like that, and faith is difficult in loneliness. I don't mean solitude, which is a good thing; I mean loneliness, which isn't. That's when one feels futility and meaninglessness haunting one. One doesn't need talk or theories or 'deep sharing' so much as the understanding presence of someone who shares one's thoughts and vision, with whom one can be natural and unguarded, whose faith and goals are the same. A friend is not someone with 'answers' for your every problem, or 'advice' for your every struggle. A friend is someone who is for another, as Aristotle said and as St. Gregory Nazianzen repeated concerning his friend St. Basil, as 'one soul existing in two bodies.' That's a matter of presence, not verbiage."

John looked at Solrunn from the other side of the table and said, "A sense of meaninglessness exists in absence; it *is* absence. God gives us particular friends to give us presence — a 'real presence' — but a presence that is particularly suited to each one of us as we are in our own personalities. But every mortal friend is just that — mortal. Friends will die, and some may leave for other demanding reasons in their lives; and we know the pain of this fact of life. Still, God provides, often quite unexpectedly."

Father Haire, seated where the hearth cast a great golden radiance (he had just put another log on the fire), nodded at John's words. "Speaking of which," he said, "let me go back to the subject of the relationship of *agape* and *philia,* and consider the Gospel in which friendship is, in fact, highlighted.

"John's Gospel is the Gospel that tells us something concrete about the role of friendship in Christ's life. It's striking to consider this in light of Jesus' more general hesitancy to entrust himself to the vast majority of his hearers. Do you recall what the Gospel tells us about this?" Father Haire flipped through the pages of his Bible, found his text, and read: "'Now when he was in Jerusalem at the Passover feast, many believed (*episteusan,* or 'put their faith') in his name when they saw the signs which he did; but Jesus *did not trust (episteuen) himself to them,* because he knew all men and needed no one to bear witness of man; for he himself knew what was in man' (John 2:23-25). So, friendship for Jesus has a meaning that includes some depth of commitment, intimacy, and even

117

mutual trust (*pistein,* or 'faith'). It's interesting that the word *faith* or *trust* is used twice. One gets the impression that Jesus is not only calling his listeners to have faith in him, but is also looking for those in whom he can have faith or trust — that is, *friends* in the truest sense. He is looking for their presence, as Solrunn has said, and certainly not their brilliant insights!

"Going a bit further in John's Gospel, we find John the Baptist saying that he is 'the *friend* of the Bridegroom' (John 3:29), a title that is more than just a title of honor, one suspects. Lazarus is 'our *friend (philos)*,' and when Jesus weeps before his tomb, those present say, 'See how he loved *(ephilei)* him!'

"It's also said straightforwardly that Jesus' love was given not only to Lazarus, but also to his sisters: 'Now Jesus loved *(egapa)* Martha and her sister and Lazarus' (John 11:5). Friendship for Jesus broke down the rigidly maintained sexual barriers of his own culture. It *is* possible in Christ for men and women to be *friends,* something that has in various contexts been forgotten, violated, repressed, held in suspicion, misunderstood, or wrongly interpreted as license for something else in the history of the church. At least in the West, the major culprit here may be St. Augustine, despite his greatness, as some have argued. Certainly his view that sin was propagated through sexuality didn't help the relations between the sexes any, increasing simultaneously both an exaggerated fear of, and consequent fascination with, sex. Nothing is sure to kill the trust and relaxed atmosphere that friendship requires than that kind of overwrought, mostly male mentality. More could be said about this subject, but we'd get too far off our topic."

Father Haire glanced at Solrunn, arms folded over her rabbit-skin vest, and then at Mother Catherine Grace. He seemed slightly unsure whether or not he had spoken inappropriately in their presence, but, reassured, he continued.

"When Christ teaches his disciples to love *(agapate)* one another as he has loved them, he goes on to tell them that they are no longer to be called servants, those who don't know what their master is up to. Instead, the revelation he has committed to them makes them his *friends (philoi),* and their friendship with him is vitally connected to obedience to his commandments (John 15:12-17).

"This is *agape,* of course, but it is something more — something more specific, something based on shared objectives, shared suffering (as John 16, for instance, makes clear), and shared struggles. It is *philia* with and in Christ, a fellowship that will grow and include others (John 17:20; 1 John 1:3)."

Father Haire paused, sipping his wine. The fire's light was slowly beginning to give way to semi-darkness.

"Yes. Lazarus," remarked John thoughtfully, then said no more. For a few moments we listened to the wind outside, and the creaking of tree limbs arching unseen above the roof of the Hermitage. Jerome, pencil in hand, was sketching Mother Catherine Grace's portrait on a small pad in his hand. He always concentrated better while he sketched.

"It is John 21, and Peter's reclamation, that intrigues me," Father Haire suddenly went on after the lengthy silence. "It has often been noted how the words *agape* and *philia* are interspersed in 21:15-17, and there have been conjectures as to whether these words are to be understood as synonymous or not. Perhaps they are to some extent, as in John 15:13 ('Greater love — *agapen* — hath no man than this, that a man lay down his life for his friends — *philon*; KJV), but notice that the 'greater love' of *agape* is in fact understood here precisely in terms of *philia*.

"Earlier in the Gospel, Peter had said this to Jesus, who had just spoken of his coming death and given the commandment for his disciples to love one another 'as I have loved you': 'Lord, why cannot I follow thee now? I will lay down my life for thy sake' (John 13:37, KJV). At which point Jesus tells Peter that he will deny him three times. Christian love is defined by Christ as willingness even to 'lay down one's life' for one's friends, something that Peter overconfidently claimed to possess, and then failed miserably to show in the courtyard of Caiaphas.

"John 21:15-17 redeems those three terrible denials with three confessions and three demands. Here's the passage. See how the words play out, keeping St. Aelred's distinction between the more general *agape* and the more particular *philia* in mind:

> So when they had dined, Jesus saith to Simon Peter, Simon, son of Jonas, lovest *(agapas)* thou me more than these? He saith unto him, Yea, Lord; thou knowest that I love *(philo)* thee. He saith unto him, Feed my lambs. He saith to him again the second time, Simon, son of Jonas, lovest *(agapas)* thou me? He saith unto him, Yea, Lord; thou knowest that I love *(philo)* thee. He saith unto him, Feed my sheep. He saith unto him the third time, Simon, son of Jonas, lovest *(phileis)* thou me? Peter was grieved because he said unto him the third time, Lovest *(phileis)* thou me? And he said unto him, Lord, thou knowest all things; thou knowest that I love *(philo)* thee. Jesus saith unto him, Feed my sheep. (KJV)

"You will note that Peter was 'grieved' or (better) 'distressed' when Jesus moved from using the word *agape* to the more pointed *philia*. Peter had been protesting all along that his love for Christ was one of 'friendship' *(philia),* even though Jesus was using the less intimate word, *agape.* When Jesus asks Peter *the third time,* and compounds this near repetition by switching to the word *philia,* two memories must have instantly surfaced in Peter's mind: his three denials of Christ after professing his willingness to lay down his life for him (13:37), and the subsequent definition of Christ that friendship means precisely such a ready willingness (15:13). No wonder Peter was pained by these memories, and we see in him the pain felt by every sincere penitent, the sorrow of every Christian who sins against the love of Christ."

At that moment I felt a keen stab in my own heart. "Sin jeopardizes our friendship with Christ," said Jerome softly. All I could manage was a nod.

Father Haire went on: "And Peter then hears from Jesus the merciful call to follow him afresh, and that he will indeed one day lay down his life for his Lord. Peter, true to form, immediately wishes to know what the future holds for the Apostle John as well; but Jesus rebukes him by saying, 'If I will that he tarry till I come, what is that to thee? Follow thou me' (John 21:18-23, KJV). With these words we see the priority of *individual* friendship *with* Christ over friendship *in* Christ. Like the 'lines' of St. Dorotheos's great circle, the center of which is God, the lines of our individual lives, as they relate to and in

Christ, should not interfere with another's unique call to discipleship, even though, in God's providence, they must all converge in him.

"This, as John said, is perhaps the most painful part of friendship or of any kind of mortal love. Friends sometimes must leave us, some die . . ."

"Lazarus," said John. There was a pause of some moments' length as we all waited to hear what was on John's mind, but he hesitated to speak. I recall now that it was getting increasingly difficult to see either John or Father Haire in the darkness. I could see Jerome, who was seated nearest me, plainly enough in the candlelight, and Mother Catherine Grace and Solrunn, but the other two men almost seemed to be fading into the shadows.

The wind had died down, and through the ice-glazed windows one could only just make out those branches closest to the panes. Dirk the dog had evidently left the room without my noticing.

John spoke again, and it seemed as if his voice was coming from all points of the room at once, filling it; and now I couldn't make him out across the table at all.

"Lazarus was the friend of Christ," he was saying, "and we see how greatly his death affected him. Christ knows grief. When death touched his friend, Christ grieved for him, and then raised him. I believe — I know — that to

Christ all of us are 'Lazarus.' His friends are those whom he will raise and bring, through the power of his own resurrection and victory over death, to share his glory. *When I died, I knew this.*"

These strange, unexpected words were like an electric shock, and Jerome and I shot wide-eyed glances at one another. Mother Catherine Grace only smiled, and Solrunn, removing her glasses, brushed her fingers against her eyes. Before our minds could assimilate these words' full import, however, Father Haire seamlessly continued John's line of thought.

"But, in Christ, the death or departure of friends is not the death of their friendship," he said. His voice, like John's, filled the room, though he was now entirely invisible to my eyes. "Just remember those words of St. Jerome, which St. Aelred liked to quote: *Friendship which can end was never true friendship.*"[8]

When one awakes from a particularly deep and dream-filled sleep, it is often difficult to remember immediately what has gone on in the waking world. With some mental effort one gropes for one's memory, and groggily recovers those facts and details that we tend to accept as reality. This began to happen to me now.

8. St. Aelred of Rievaulx, *Spiritual Friendship,* 1:68; also 1:24.

First, I heard Jerome's voice say, "I remember. John did die. It was sudden. And Father Haire died nearly thirty years ago. . . ."

And as he said this, I felt sharply the loss of these friends anew.

It was with this lingering sense — a curious mixture of absence and presence — that I awoke.

Later that day, I phoned Jerome and Mother Catherine Grace, both a thousand miles away from where I lived. Then I phoned Solrunn, nearly five times that distance away. To each I recounted the dream and spoke of old times in the light of eternity.

Chapter Seven

Concluding Unscientific Postscript

T HIS BOOK has actually been about faith throughout. *Faith* is a word often misunderstood, even by those professing it.

For some, "faith" means something akin to optimism. Someone with faith is not supposed to have doubts or sorrows. It is confused with "positive thinking" and cheerfulness and unquestioning assurance. A high priority is placed on having "correct feelings."

For others, "faith" means intellectual assent to a systematic body of doctrine, a tough-minded and unwavering adherence to abstract concepts and cast-iron dogmas. The priority here is on "correct thinking."

For still others, mainly for those who reject it, "faith" is looked upon as almost the very opposite of reason — as an intellectually vapid submissiveness to some brand or other of religious authority in matters no one could ever rationally prove to be true. "Faith" is a "blind leap" into something irrational, probably superstitious, and easily ridiculed. Whether it's "faith" in fairies, or in the miraculous intervention of Our Lady of Fatima, or in the existence of God, it is all the same to them. In other words, faith is confused with simple-mindedness and credulity. But, at the same time, it's not at least charitably considered to be naïve. Instead, it's often linked by those who claim to be "rationally minded" to bigotry, arrogance, and violence (as if "faith" actually breeds these things naturally, and not something else in the human condition). As Christopher Hitchens puts it, "religion kills," and it "poisons everything." By this estimation, "faith" is deemed a kind of primitive prejudice in favor of what one merely wants to believe. It belongs to the "babyhood" of human evolution.

But all such notions of faith are mistaken. Faith is not good feelings. It isn't rationalism. Nor is it superstition. All these interpretations suffer from a single underlying error. Faith is not something static and flat, and yet every one of these interpretations assumes that it is. So, for instance, one has "faith" *or* one is unhappy; or, one has "faith" *or* one is heterodox; or, one has "faith" *or* one is rational. Faith in each case means a static, flat *something* with which one can contrast a static, flat *something else.*

Faith, in other words, *just is*. "It" is thus conveniently categorized. "It" is either correct or incorrect, and either one has "it" or one doesn't. Very easy, very cut-and-dried, and seemingly everyone knows what is being talked about when the word *faith* is mentioned in a given context. And so it is that few definitions are apparently ever required.

However, faith is not so easily understood as all that.

For someone who considers faith a matter of positive feelings, we see instead that faith can also include *melancholy,* even depression, and "dark nights." What would a defender of "good-times faith," for example, make of the words of Johannes Tauler, the fourteenth-century Dominican mystic, who described as part of growth in faith the experience of being "abandoned [by God] in such a way that we no longer have any knowledge of God and we fall into such anguish so as not to know any more if we were ever on the right path, nor do we know if God does or does not exist, or if we are alive or dead . . ."? Faith, far from encouraging any dependence on feelings for the sake of one's self-assurance, rather crucifies such emotional dependence.

For those who think that faith is all about having the right theology, we find that *skepticism* is a usefully critical aspect of faith. In Christianity especially, where the cross is the central symbol, faith crucifies neat abstractions and the arrogance of our intellect. Faith as manifested in the cross of Jesus isn't reducible to *an idea.*

For those who think that faith is essentially in opposition to reason, all one can reasonably conclude is that for them, unlike most of the human race, faith remains simply a mystery altogether. Those who profess to have no faith really have nothing much of any profundity to say on the subject itself, even if they sometimes make the occasional valid point about others who do profess it. They are assessing faith with an instrument not adequate for the job. And, of course, for them the cross, as the existential focal point of faith, is — as St. Paul says of the philosophical Greeks — "foolishness." We can only just leave them in that assumption. Argument about such a subject would be a waste of effort.

Faith is not static or flat. That must be asserted forcefully. It is dynamic and has height and depth and length and width. It is living, growing, changing, and it is integral to a human being's very existence and maturing. It isn't measurable by human ingenuity. It is vast, all-encompassing. No one can do an experiment on it, like some have tried to do with "faith healing" and intercessory prayer for the sick. It is *atmospheric* for those who live in it, not one closet among many inside oneself. One grows within the atmosphere of faith, and it is — to use Blake's language — a cleansing of "the doors of perception." Even when someone with faith temporarily lacks any sense of its presence, it is nonetheless *there* in the very desire to sense it.

It is a form of inherent "trust," and a "feeling" (as Schleiermacher used the word) that all things are imbued with, or resting upon, or embraced by, "something" infinite, mysterious, sacred: *mysterium tremendum fascinans et augustum* (Rudolf Otto). It is the universally experienced insight that God "is not far from each one of us, for 'In him we live and move and have our being'" (Acts 17:27-28; Paul is apparently quoting Epimenides).

Humanity has always existed in the atmosphere of faith as fish do in water. Even before we begin to consider a specific focus for it, we should at least acknowledge that without faith there would be no art, no science, no pursuit of knowledge and understanding whatsoever. It is *faith* — trust in what is perceived, trust in the universe's essential sacredness — that gives us the basic notion that there is something to be understood or appreciated or fashioned or loved at all. Faith is what distinguishes the human consciousness from that of the other animals.

At this point it is sincerely to be doubted that even those who deny having faith are wholly without it. Why would anyone, for instance, ever bother with anything so demanding and ultimately unrewarding as scientific research — there being little chance that one could ever know everything about anything in the course of a single meager lifetime — if not motivated by a *faith* that presses one on *to know?*

If it is to be questioned whether or not what I'm attempting to describe is in fact "faith," I merely ask in reply if there is any other suitable word for it, and — if so — how is it distinguishable from faith? "Curiosity" won't do the trick: what, after all, intellectively motivates human curiosity? Answer: Faith that there is *something* to be curious about — some greater mystery yet to be explored.

To go much further (skipping over many things lying in between, since this is not "an argument" but a brief "Concluding Unscientific Postscript" — with apologies to Kierkegaard), specifically Christian faith finds its focus in Jesus of Nazareth, and his followers have never forgotten that he was crucified as a common criminal — the sort of execution meted out to slaves, to those deemed "nonpersons" by the prevailing Greco-Roman world. Paul could write to the church in Corinth that he "decided to know nothing . . . except Jesus Christ and him crucified" (1 Cor. 2:2).

For the early Christians, the sign of the cross was a sign of defiance — in the very depths, in the gutters of human life, among the slaves and the poor and those crushed, in the darkness, God had made himself present.

Even there, not only in the "sacred" places — the Roman temples and groves and monuments and consecrated altars and cultic fripperies — the sacred had manifested itself. Not only in nature, not only in the presence of the awesome and frighteningly majestic, but among the wretched and unclean, God had revealed himself. And even where death was most horrifically displayed — the cross, as the ancient Roman world saw it before the fourth century, and not the gold and bejeweled crosses of later triumphal Christendom — even there appeared the promise of resurrection and life.

Admittedly, this faith is something more demanding and even more all-encompassing than the sort of atmospheric faith integral to humanity in general. It embraces both the sacred and the profane. An instrument of torture, a symbol of an empire's methodical way of dealing with its poorest malefactors and rebels, becomes the defiant symbol of a peaceful revolt right under the very nose of worldly power. Faith is no longer merely atmospheric, but volitional and vigorous, willing to love even enemies in the face of hatred and die at their hands in the face of threat. The cross as the Christians' central sign, utilizing the very image of threat established by the rulers and military to intimidate them, was in effect saying, "We take up the cross — *your sign* of domination and coercion. We take it from now on as *our sign*. If you strike us on the right cheek, we will present to you the left one as well. You can butcher us, but we won't back down. *Jesus, whom you crucified, whom God raised from the dead and exalted to his 'right hand' — not Caesar — is Lord...."*

SO IT IS that the faithful Christian is not ultimately afraid of the reality of melancholy and darkness. He knows that God has left no one utterly at the mercy of darkness. If there is a cross, there is also resurrection. He can know his own darkness in the hope that there he will meet with the Christ who suffered, was depressed, grieved, wept, and died in torment. Even though he should become an a-theist for a time, saying, "My God, my God, why have you forsaken me?" he knows that he is in the same darkness that God inhabits. In that encounter he will also know that faith — trust — in the midst of darkness is transfiguring, and even perhaps a necessity for him. Someone who has experienced it can certainly learn compassion for others' darkness in such a crucible.

Neither does the faithful Christian flinch before skepticism. Skepticism will always preserve him from the false forms of "faith" mentioned above — the emotionally dependent, the rationalistic, the irrational and superstitious. It will also preserve him from the sort of perennial popular and philosophical atheism that has plenty of argument and rebuttal, but not much else. Skepticism will always doubt the value of doubt itself, because doubt — as opposed to faith — explains nothing about the most essential mystery of humanity. After all, religion doesn't "kill" or "poison" anything; human beings at their worst do that, and they do it to and with religion just as surely as they do it to and with everything else of value, including science.

Lastly, an unutterably splendid gift that Christ gives his friends is friends. Authentic friendship will always be a greater force and source of strength than empires, political parties, nationalities, fellowships, institutions, or anything else of human social invention. It has the power to overthrow and cast down those things that would do the same to us psychologically, emotionally, physically, or spiritually.

A true friend in Christ will be there in the darkness with us if need be; and may we all learn to be such friends to others. There are few callings in life so noble and worthy. It is an imitation of Christ.

O my Master, O my Master!
He judges the ten thousand things — all of life —
*   but he doesn't think himself a judge.*
His blessings extend to ten thousand generations
*   — all of life — but he doesn't think himself*
*   as blessed.*

Concluding Unscientific Postscript

He is older than the highest antiquity, but he
doesn't think himself old.
Overarching heaven, bearing up the earth and
forming all things, but he doesn't think
himself skilled.
It is through him — with him — that I wander.

Chuang Tzu,
fourth century B.C.

Acknowledgments

Unless otherwise noted, the Scripture quotations in this publication are from the Revised Standard Version of the Bible, copyrighted 1946, 1952 © 1971, 1973 by the Division of Christian Education of the National Council of Churches of Christ in the U.S.A., and used by permission.

Cistercian Publications has granted permission to reprint quotations from St. Aelred of Rievaulx's *Spiritual Friendship,* translated by M. E. Laker and published by Cistercian Publications in 1974.

Faber & Faber, Ltd., has granted permission to reprint quotations from *Early Fathers from the Philokalia,* translated by Eugenia Kadloubovsky and G. E. H. Palmer and published by Faber & Faber, Ltd., in 1954.